REDZONE RETIREMENT PLAN

A Playbook
to Executing Your Ideal Retirement

Adam Olson

REDZONE RETIREMENT PLAN
Copyright © 2023 Adam Olson
All Rights Reserved

This book or any portion thereof may not be reproduced or used in any manner whatsoever without the express written permission of the publisher except in the case of reprints in the context of reviews, quotes, or references.

Limit of Liability/Disclaimer of Warranty. While the publisher and author have used their best efforts in preparing this book, they make no representation or warranties with respect to the accuracy or completeness of the contents of this book. (The author and/or publisher do not guarantee that anyone following these strategies, suggestions, ideas, will be successful. The advice and strategies contained herein may not be suitable for your situation. You should consult with a professional where appropriate. Neither the publisher nor author shall be liable for any loss of profit or any other commercial damage including, but not limited to, special, incidental, consequential, or other damages.)

Printed in the United States of America
ISBN- 978-1-953497-49-9 (Print)
ISBN- 978-1-953497-50-5 (Digital)

Library of Congress Control Number: 2023901082

Published by Cocoon to Wings Publishing
7810 Gall Blvd. #311
Zephyrhills, FL 33541
www.CocoontoWingsBooks.com
(813) 906-WING (9464)

**Financial statement images presented as resource information in this book are used with written permission from both © Advisys Inc. 2023 and Wealth2k, Inc. Copyright 2004-2022 Wealth2k, Inc. All Rights Reserved. The Income for Life Model® is a registered trademark of Wealth2k, Inc.

Cover design by ETP Creative

REDZONE RETIREMENT PLAN

Adam Olson

ACKNOWLEDGEMENTS

A big THANK YOU to Stephanie Outten for her guidance and support in assisting me with this, my third book. Stephanie's partnership has done more for my business growth than she will ever know. I pray for continued blessings to her and the Cocoon to Wings Publishing team. Stephanie, I look forward to working with you on more projects in the future.

I would also like to thank Ereka Thomas for her creative design for this newest book. She was able – again - to take a jumbled thought in my mind and turn it into something beautiful. Ereka is a true artist.

Next, thank you to Emily Claudette Freeman for her numerous hours of work trying to decipher my jumbled writings into the final book that you have here. Thank you for your patience and guidance in our collaboration.

Lastly, I want to thank my family: Katie, Hudson, Kiptyn, and Tate. You all are the reason I get up every morning. Katie, you push me to be a better person in every area of my life. And my boys are the reason I want to be the best Christian father that I can be.

CONTENTS

Acknowledgements iv

Preface: Why? ix

Introduction 1

PART 1: WHAT YOU NEED TO THINK ABOUT

Chapter 1 – What are you retiring to? Purpose. 17

Chapter 2 – Dreams and Goals 25

Chapter 3 – Lifestyle 35

Chapter 4 – Phased retirement, part-time work 43

PART 2: WHAT YOU NEED TO DO

Chapter 5 – How Much $ Do I Need? 57

Chapter 6 – Creating your distribution strategy 65

Chapter 7 – Investing Strategies 71

Chapter 8 – Leaving a Legacy 79

PART 3: WHAT YOU NEED TO KNOW

Chapter 9 – Social Security 91

Chapter 10 – The Medicare Maze 101

Chapter 11 – Long-Term Care Planning 109

Chapter 12 – Estate Planning 119

Chapter 13 – Taxes 127

Chapter 14 – Picking your team 145

Appendix 170

PREFACE: WHY?

I have three young boys, and most days I get the age-old question asked trillions of times by kids around the world, "But why, Dad?"

Most of the time my response is, "That is just the way it is," or "Just because."

Which leads to another question from them, "why?"

But sometimes when they ask, "But why, Dad?" they have a good question that I must think about before I can produce an answer. Kids question everything, and sometimes they need to learn from their own mistakes. I could tell my kids dozens of times not to touch the toaster because they will get burned, but sometimes they must get hurt to learn.

Hopefully, we are more adapted to learning without pain as adults, and we can learn from others' mistakes. Still, I do love (some days) the way kids question everything. This book is designed to help you create your own "RedZone Retirement Plan," and part of that is questioning everything that you think you know about traditional retirement. I find "that's just the way it is" is not a response that we should readily accept in most areas of our life ESPECIALLY when it comes to retirement planning. My kids never accept "that's just the way it is" as an answer, and neither should you.

Here are some questions I want you to ponder about retirement:

1. Why do we still have retirement ages?
2. Why haven't these changed much over the years?
3. What/who does your retirement hurt?
4. How would the world look if no one retired?
5. What are the sad and lonely parts of retirement?
6. What do you lose in retirement?
7. Where does your purpose come from in retirement?
8. What are your retirement rights?
9. Why retire?

These questions do not have a right or wrong answer. There is not one single definition of a successful retirement, everyone's dream retirement looks different. I pose them to help you start to think differently about retirement, and to question where your real retirement dreams lie. These dreams and desires are YOURS; don't let society tell you what a happy retirement is.

You can define that for yourself.

Most retirees' biggest fear is running out of money, which is why Certified Financial Planners (CFPs), like me, are in business. We keep people's fears from becoming a reality. This book gives you the tools and knowledge to make sure that running out of money is very unlikely.

BUT is that really a retiree's biggest fear?

What most retirees don't think about is running out of **purpose, good health, time, friends,** and **family**. These are some of the biggest issues in retirement that no one ever talks about, and what I want to focus a large part of the book on. Honestly, it would be a sad world for you if every single one of your friends and family members were dead and gone, along with your spouse. This is a real fear that we need to address for you. We will do this in this book by digging into what your true passions are and enabling you to fulfill those early and often.

Money is PART of your retirement plan, yes, a big part, but not the whole part. I need you to focus on your *whole self* when creating your "RedZone Retirement Plan."

Don't be afraid to ask "why?" and **don't** answer a question with, "that is just the way it is." You are in control of your retirement plan. Let's start to create that plan right now.

INTRODUCTION

I grew up and live in Nebraska where football (to some) is a religion, and with a title like "The RedZone Retirement Plan" you might think that I am a HUGE football fan. Spoiler alert, I'm not.

But I did play football my senior year of high school. I was not a huge pick up for the team, and the cross-country team didn't suffer a huge loss when I left to join the football team. I was not fast, which is important in football, and I really didn't have much endurance, which is essential in cross-country. In cross-country meets we would run 3.1 miles, and most courses have two to four loops. These loops are long, and as a runner it's very rare to get lapped in a meet. Well, my brother did just that to me one time. Yes, he lapped me in a cross-country race. The sad part is he didn't even say anything as he ran by. He just kept on running. If I could have caught my breath I would have at least said, "Good job, buddy."

As I said, I wasn't a huge pick up for the football team either. I vividly remember playing on the defensive line in our first game of that season. One of our coaches (Mr. Mac) was screaming at me the whole first series, "ADAM, shoot the A gap, SHOOT THE A GAP."

After we got off the field, he grabbed me and pulled me aside and asked, "Why aren't you listening to me out there?"

My response was, "Coach I have no idea what 'shoot the A gap' means."

In football, when a coach says shoot the gap, they want you to work the space between the offensive and defensive linemen. Coaches give gaps letters dependent upon a player's distance from the center. So, in yelling for me to shoot the A gap, he was hoping I would work the space between the center and the guard.

It was a rough football career for me. But I did manage to catch a two-point conversion one time! Please don't worry, I'm a way better financial planner than athlete. I've found my niche in the finance world.

If you are hoping this whole book is filled with sports metaphors about football, it's not. But what you will find is **everything** that you need to know about how to create your ideal retirement. I simply liken the

RedZone football comparison to my RedZone Retirement plan comparison below.

The RedZone in football, from what I'm told, is where you get close to the endzone (20 yards out to be exact). When you get close, it gets VERY important that you execute so that you can score a touchdown (7 points). If you don't score a touchdown, you could always kick a field goal (3 points). If neither of those things happen, you will end up giving the ball back to the other team. Leaving the RedZone without a score is devastating and can leave a team feeling defeated.

In retirement, the RedZone that I refer to is five to eight years out from your retirement date, and the first five to eight years into your retirement. This is where it gets EXTREMELY important that you plan and prepare for your eventual retirement. Every decision that you make at this point can have life and retirement altering consequences. If you take too much out or invest too aggressively you could run out of money in the future. Which is WAY worse than not scoring a touchdown.

Your Retirement Redzone is the most dangerous time in your investing life. If you retire into a down market and you are not adequality prepared with cash reserves, you could run the risk of running out of money. *Sequence of Return Risk* or *Timing Risk* is a very dangerous part of retirement. We will dig into these terms more.

Just like in football, in retirement you can:

Get a touchdown: Retire one time with a perfect plan in place, hit all your goals, and live an amazing, stress-free life.

Get a field goal: Not a perfectly executed plan, but you are able to retire and stay retired. You may have to make some sacrifices and alter your goals.

Lose the ball: If this happens in retirement you may have to re-enter the workforce unwillingly. Or you may have to drastically alter your retirement plan, changing your lifestyle to fit your budget.

I know I was not good at football. But I am good at educating you about decisions you will need to make for your future retirement and giving you all the plays that you will need to run to WIN the game of retirement.

Nick Saban, who is a pretty good football coach, has said, "we practice until we can't get it wrong." This is a whole different mentality than the traditional saying, "let's practice until we get it right." Saban's mentality is what you need as you plan and prepare for your retirement. That is the way that I think about retirement planning for my clients. We have ONE chance to do this right, so let's make sure we make the proper decisions that will result in a successful retirement.

In football there are risks when you enter the red zone; you could fumble, throw an interception, or turn it over on downs. Similarly, you have risks when you enter retirement such as: retiring in a down stock market, running out of money, and ending up in a nursing home. Having a RedZone plan is key to executing in either situation.

> *"If you fail to plan, you are planning to fail."* ~ **Benjamin Franklin, Founding father of the United States**

This book is broken into three parts.

Part 1: What you need to think about.

This is a higher-level thinking section of the book. Here you will imagine what your ideal retirement looks like, and it will give you things to consider when you are in the planning stage for it. If you don't have a plan, you will likely not live your best days in that post-career and post-child rearing life phase. This is just like a football team watching film of the team they are playing in the next game. They study their opposition, so they have a game plan to success, you need to study for your retirement, so you have a game plan to enjoy it successfully.

Part 2: What you need to do.

This section is where you will get concrete action steps to take toward executing your retirement plan; and guidance on how you can do this yourself or find a professional to work with. Part 2 is where you will create your personal "RedZone Retirement Playbook." Take the information from this part to create and execute your plan.

Part 3: What you need to know.

You always save the best part for last. This section will walk you through the nuts and bolts of retirement and give you a basic understanding of all the different financial aspects of retirement. I'll walk you through Medicare and Social Security, and much more. Some of this will get into the weeds a little bit, so stick to the highlights if you want a general grasp of each topic. You must know some of these basic retirement concepts to think about and plan for your future.

Some people manage their retirement planning and investments by themselves. They are disciplined enough to do it on their own, and they are educated enough to make all the right decisions. Most importantly they have the TIME and PASSION to do it right. If this is you, this book will help you with the decisions you will need to make to create your retirement plan.

And it will give you strategies to implement to put your plan in place.

If that is NOT you, that is okay. I do have some good news for you, people like me exist to help people like you.

I'm a Certified Financial Planner (CFP) and every single day I walk my clients to and through retirement. With the planning that I do with my clients we consider all aspects of your retirement life when creating your personalized retirement plan, not just your investment portfolio. My team and I consider every single part of your retirement plan from investments to taxes, and even your Medicare and lifestyle choices. My goal is for you to never have to work a day longer than necessary. The process involves a TON of planning, though, and is a decision that is not made in one day.

As a financial professional, I work as a fiduciary for my investment advisory clients. This means I treat all clients' accounts as if they were my own. I put myself in my clients' shoes every day, and I make suggestions for them as if it were my own account. There are thousands of CFP professionals like me around the country with whom you can work. You can find one at letsmakeaplan.org.

If you need help, or a simple financial health check in, I would be happy to consult with you. My business website is adamolson.biz, and my email address is *adam.olson@mutualofomaha.com*.

I'm passionate about educating everyone at any age about all things personal finance related and equipping them to make smart financial decisions. My first book, "21 Things You Need to Know About Money," is a beginner's guide to finances. When I speak to high school students, most with zero understanding about money, I give them this book. It's a great starter's guide to personal finance. It covers everything from budgeting, to loans, to investment accounts.

My second book, "What's Your Plan?" builds on the first book and gives advice and guidance to readers about creating a financial plan or a roadmap to retirement. It covers topics like where and how to save for your future retirement and digs into how much you should be saving. This book is designed to enable readers to effectively plan for their financial future. Both books can be found on Amazon.com.

If you are a pre-retiree and you do not understand basic principles of personal finance, this book is going to be extremely confusing to you. You MUST have a general understanding of pre-tax versus post-tax accounts, brokerage accounts, investment risk and diversification, and insurance (health, life, long term care). If these concepts are foreign to you, please check out my first two books as resources to get you up to speed.

In addition, if you are struggling with debt and budgeting, please consider reading my first two books as a prerequisite BEFORE you start this one. You can't run before you can walk, and you can't plan for your retirement if you can't run a budget.

Before we start, I do need to add that if you are married then you should be reading this, and having these financial planning conversations, with your spouse. If you and your spouse are not on the same page, you will be very disappointed when you have differing interests and passions in retirement.

Get ready and prepare to enter…

"The Retirement RedZone"

PART 1

WHAT YOU NEED TO THINK ABOUT

I'm sure you have seen the ads "You need $1,000,000 to retire happy," or "Retirement today requires $1,000,000." Let me tell you, there are people that retire happy and love their life with only $200,000. And there are people who retire with $5,000,000 and are miserable. It all comes down to what you want, doing that within your financial abilities, and finding happiness in that.

Let me add that if you only have $100,000 saved for retirement but you want to live a retirement like you have $1,000,000 saved, you may need to tone down your expectations.

Most things take money, and you CANNOT earn your way out of a spending deficit in retirement. If you are retired, your income is cut off, so you must stick within your spending limits in retirement. This is not a situation like you may have had in your 30's where you can take on some debt and spending habits and still recover. Sticking to your plan in retirement is a necessity and spending too much, too early, can have life-altering effects.

In this first part of the book, we need to start dreaming about your future. If you don't have a plan for what your future retirement is going to look like, you will be disappointed with what it looks like. Planning for your retirement can't be done in one day. This will be an ongoing conversation that you will be having to mold your future into what you want it to be.

Far too many people yearn for retirement only to get there and be disappointed with their lifestyle.

Why?

Well, it is simply because they never imagined what they wanted their future to look like. They never put any time into planning what they would be doing in retirement. It is very important to find what makes you happy and focus on that. For some, that may mean being close to family, for others it may mean being as far away from family as possible. For some, it may be golfing every day, others may love to garden, or go fishing. Some people may want to travel the world, others may just want to slow down and spend more time volunteering or working on passion products. Whatever it is you want to do, make sure you are doing it because it is something that you enjoy.

Some very important things for retirement happiness are having a steady paycheck, having guaranteed income, no debt, sufficient cash reserves, and staying active and healthy. Relationships and purpose are also very important things that you need to have in retirement. We will dig into these things more in this part.

As you are thinking through your future, I want you to remember these phases in retirement: Go-Go years, Slow-Go years, and your No-Go years. These are the different phases that you will go through in retirement.

Go-Go Years:

These are your first 10 years of retirement, when you are still healthy and have energy. The Go-Go Years are when you will be doing the most from being active, to traveling, to being involved in your community. It is also the phase that you will spend the most time in.

One question I love to ask clients when we are talking about these Go-Go years is,

> "What would you do If you were told you only have 5-10 years to live, but your health is going to be great during that time?"

This helps put things into perspective for you, helping you to realize that, in the future, you will not be able to do the things you once could. Do the things you have always wanted to do during these Go-Go years.

Slow-Go years:

This is usually years 10-20 of your retirement. This is when your spending and activity starts to slow down usually from your health slowly deteriorating and not having the same energy that you did in the Go-Go years. In these years, retirees tend to travel less and spend more time in their homes.

No-Go Years:

This is 20 years and more into your retirement, where your morning coffee with your crew is usually the highlight of the day. You cannot get around like you could have 20 years ago, and due to your health issues, you can't travel and be as active as you used to.

As you get further into your retirement, your spending on fun and entertainment will slow down. So, please plan to do some of the things that you want to do in your retirement in your early years. Don't save that trip around the world for your 85th birthday when you may not be able to enjoy it like you could have when you were 65.

The one potential expense that could significantly increase in retirement is your health care costs, and the possibility of moving into a nursing facility. I want to reinforce that you need to have a plan for that.

Also, in this part, we will drill down into what your **wants**, **needs**, and **fears** are. If you know what these are, you will be able to address these BEFORE you retire to make all your retirement dreams come true.

Let's dig into Part 1 and start *dreaming* about your future!

CHAPTER 1

WHAT ARE YOU RETIRING TO? PURPOSE.

> The purposes of a person's heart are deep waters, but one who has insight draws them out.
>
> PROVERBS 20:5 (NIV)

It is not an easy thing to redefine your life after retirement, and I love the way that verse from Proverbs puts it. You must think deeply about your purpose and think about it for some time before you figure out exactly what it is. For most of you, your purpose (for many years) was found in your job; this is not a bad thing at all. If you are any good at your career, it will become a part of who you are and how you identify yourself. When you retire, you must re-create yourself and find a new purpose if you want to live a happy life.

It's like the saying, "the first day a farmer dies is when he quits farming." Many farmers go to the grave farming; they can't and won't imagine their life without it.

Re-defining your purpose in retirement, which isn't easy, is a huge key to having happiness and feeling content in retirement. You almost must become a whole new person. Think of it as reinventing yourself.

The best example I can think of is Saul becoming Apostle Paul in the Bible. He flipped from persecuting Christians to converting people to Christianity. Hopefully, you're not persecuting anyone pre-retirement, but you still may need to do some reinventing of yourself in your retirement years if you want to truly find your purpose.

Sitting on your couch for years on end in retirement is not going to be good for you. Also, on the other side, sitting on a beach drinking and doing nothing for years on end is not going to be a good thing either. Retirement life needs to have a balance between freedom to do the things that you want to do for yourself, and time where you are still being a contributing member in your community (serving a purpose). You need to find things to fill up your time, that keep you healthy and active.

I personally find myself being the most unproductive on the days when I do not have anything to do. On these rare days, I won't wake up as early, I won't work out right away, and I never get as much done. On the other side, if I have a busy day I'm up early, my workout is done first thing, and I can get many things done before lunch.

Imagine if every day I woke up I had nothing to do and nothing on my schedule. I would sleep in late, watch a ton of TV, and gain 30 pounds in the first month. That is painful for me to think about, and honestly would be a sad life to live. We DO NOT want that to be your retirement. So here are some things that you need to think about and consider when re-defining yourself after retirement.

Hobbies are one of the most important things that you can have in retirement. If those hobbies involve some physical activity and social aspect, all the better. If you have the daily hobby of sitting in a casino or closing the bar down every night, those might not be the best hobbies to have for your health and wealth.

Hobbies

Hobbies that keep you social, active, and give you something to look forward to, are ones that you want to do. These are some of the great things that you should consider doing in retirement: Golfing, exercise classes, walking, biking, fishing, hunting, etc. Even things that keep your mind sharp are excellent as well, think about book clubs, card clubs, and social clubs, for example.

Finding your favorite healthy hobbies and doing them on a regular basis is something that you should plan to do in retirement. Hobbies are certainly something that you can be passionate about and sharing that passion with others is a great way for you to find purpose and happiness in retirement.

I know my grandpa loved to golf and fish, and I have many fond memories of him sharing those passions with me. Even though he may not have been the best golfer or fisher, we spent quite a bit of time doing these things together and we had a blast. Sadly, I never got the chance to ask him, but I would imagine every time we had an outing on the schedule, he looked forward to it and it may have been the highlight of his day. I'm sure he would say that was part of his purpose in retirement.

If you are married, think about if your hobbies are something you want to do with or without your spouse. Some spouses do everything together in retirement and have a great relationship, others see each other about as much as when they were working and have a great relationship. Everyone is different; you need to keep that in mind when you are deciding what will work for you in your retirement.

Volunteer Work

Volunteering is another huge thing that should be part of your retirement plan. Whether it is at your church, local school, or with a community organization, this is something you should be considering. Most communities have a huge need for volunteers, you could fill some of those needs while adding to your purpose. You have a lifetime of experience and knowledge, keeping all of that to yourself and not sharing it is a huge waste.

Get out there and get involved and help the future generation to be better than you were. Having something to do and having people that depend on you will give you a new purpose. When you do something that you find value in then everyone can benefit. You are helping others out, while serving a purpose. Depending on what you volunteer for, it will also have a social aspect to it as well, which – again - is key to having a fulfilling retirement. Where you want to volunteer and what you want to do should be something that you are considering in retirement.

Relationships

Relationships are something that most of us, unfortunately, take for granted. However, during the COVID shutdown, we all found a new appreciation for relationships. We, as human beings, are social animals, some of us more than others. It is extremely important for you in retirement to continue to be around people, and not become a hermit. Be active, be social, continue to be around others, and build new relationships as well. Don't forget to be around younger people. We reflect those we surround ourselves with. As a retiree, if the only people you associate with are sluggish, pessimistic, tired, and bored, what do you think you are going to be? Stay young, stay active, stay social.

You can't buy your health. You have probably heard that thousands of times. But it is true, if you don't have your health in retirement, you don't have much. Keeping active and healthy is going to allow you to be able to enjoy life to the fullest during retirement. Having a daily plan to be active will not only keep you healthy, but it can also save on health care costs.

It is crazy to me the amount of time, as well as money, that some people spend on their health care needs in retirement. I know you cannot control everything that happens to your health. We are all pre-disposed to some health issues. But we can control how much we move, how much we eat, and how we handle our preventative health care needs. Remember, "an ounce of prevention is worth a pound of cure."

Finding your purpose in retirement is going to be one of the most important parts of your plan. Figure out what you can do that will continue to give you purpose and start right now to plan how you can enhance that once you retire. If that is spending more time on your hobbies or finding a new hobby, that is great; or if it is volunteering, make it a plan. Don't forget to keep and maintain your relationships and stay active.

Write down the top 3 things that you want to focus on in retirement to give you purpose.

CHAPTER 2

DREAMS AND GOALS

> "You are never too old to set another goal or to dream a new dream."
>
> ~C.S. LEWIS~ BRITISH WRITER AND ANGELICAN LAY THEOLOGIAN

I love this C.S. Lewis quote. I can remember my grandma reading me his *Chronicles of Narnia* chapter books at nap time. Sometimes these naps never happened because we would get to a good part in the book, and I couldn't let her stop reading. My imagination would be on fire. This quote is perfect for this chapter because you should not let age deter you from setting a goal.

I'm reminded daily of the crazy imaginations that my young boys have. They come up with ideas that I would never think of. It's true that we lose the ability to dream and be creative as we age. So, put on your imagination hat and get ready to daydream about your future.

Having dreams and goals of what you want is another large part of having a fulfilling retirement. Being able to do what you want when you want is the reason you have worked your whole life, and why you want to retire in the first place.

In this chapter, we want to focus on what you want from your retirement and how you want it to look. Some of my clients want to live on a lake, fish every day in the fall, or have the time to spend a month with the grandkids. You want to travel the world, buy a sports car, or even donate your time to a charity. Some people simply want to sleep in and let life move slowly. Everyone's retirement goals are different.

Don't let other people's retirement lifestyle influence what yours is, plan to do what makes you happy in retirement. A great way to dig into your dreams and goals is to first look at what your wants, needs, and fears are.

Wants:

These are things that you *want* from your retirement but may not be requirements for you. Please dream a little bit here, think BIG. If you had a perfect retirement, what would it look like? What do you have? What would you be doing, or not doing?

Examples
Spend the winters in the south (snowbirds), take four vacations a year, travel the world, have a second home, spend more time with grandkids, get a lake home, buy a sports car, pay for the grandkids' college, start a business, move to a different home/state, have no debt, help kids with financial needs, help charities, etc.

Needs:
These are the MUST HAVES. The things you absolutely cannot live without. In retirement, think of these as your non-negotiables. Some people's wants may be your needs, and some people's needs may be your wants.

Examples
Food, shelter, clothing, maintaining your lifestyle (with memberships, organizations, sponsorships, dues). Have $____ of guaranteed income a month, have a second home, keep up your annual donations, be able to eat out, paid off home, and be able to support kids/grandkids.

Fears:

No one likes to talk about what they are afraid of. But knowing these fears and addressing them will allow you to live a free and happy retirement. When you are thinking about fears, think about what keeps you up at night. What worries you?

Examples

Running out of money, not maintaining your health, losing money in the stock market, not leaving anything behind for your kids, ending up in a nursing home, not managing your time well, losing your purpose, being bored, being lonely…

Take a minute to think about what your **wants**, **needs**, and **fears** are.

Better yet, write them down. Get your top 3 in.

Wants

_____

_____

_____

Needs

_____

_____

Fears

_____

_____

_____

Please keep these fears in mind when you are thinking about your big picture. Knowing what you are afraid of will help you decide what you want to focus on. If your biggest fear is running out of money, then you will want more guaranteed income in retirement. If your biggest fear is waiting too long to live the retirement that you want, then start doing the things that you want to sooner than later.

Now that you have thought about the big picture, let's drill down and set a few **goals** that you have for your retirement. The first goal you need to think about is, at what age do I want this to happen? Is it 62, 65, 66? At what age would you prefer to retire?

Write it down (Age____).

If you are married, spouse's retirement age (Age_____). We will drill down more in the next part to help you decide whether this is possible or not.

The next goal I like clients to set has to do with cash reserves. A great question to ask yourself is, "how much cash on hand do I need in retirement so that I'm not worried about the stock market affecting my lifestyle and my retirement income plans?" For most people this is anywhere from three months to 18 months' worth of living expenses. If you have a large amount of guaranteed income in retirement from Social Security, Pensions, Annuities, maybe your number is on the lower end (three to six months). If you have little to no guaranteed income, you may want to be on the higher end for cash reserves (12-18 months).

I can't stress this enough; you need to be aware how secure your income is. If all your income depends on the performance of the stock market, you may need more cash on hand because if the market drops by 25% you will not want to do distributions from your investments. Bottom line is everyone has an amount of cash that they need in the bank to feel secure. Think of it as multiple months of your monthly expenses and figure out the amount that is right for you. Is it three months of those expenses, six months, or nine months?

Amount of cash needed at retirement ($_____) based on what you've considered would be that amount. Set a goal to have that much accumulated in cash by your future retirement date.

Even in retirement, "Cash is KING," just like Dave Ramsey preaches.

Another goal that leads to a very happy retirement is not having any personal debt to your name. Now, this is not a requirement, and some people will argue with you that if mortgage rates are under 3% you would be stupid to not carry a mortgage in retirement.

However, we are emotional creatures, and we need to keep these emotions in check. You get a freeing feeling when you no longer have any payments to make. You are not stressed about that debt hanging over your head. And not having to worry about a payment in retirement is one less thing that you must think about coming out of your paychecks. A great future goal for you to set is to have no debt when you enter retirement. **This is a big key to retirement happiness.**

Guaranteed paychecks are the last goal that I want you to think about. You have been getting a paycheck for 30 or more years while you were working. I like clients to have the same thing in retirement. The question I want you to ask is,

"How much of my paycheck needs to be guaranteed?"

I like to think of it this way. Let's guarantee your basic living expenses (food, shelter, clothing); these would be the needs you listed above. You can get this guaranteed check through: Social Security, Pensions, Cash accounts, Annuities. What is that number for you?

All the variable expenses can be covered from a variable income source, this would be your wants. Depending on market conditions, you may not get all your wants. Having a guaranteed paycheck makes your financial life less stressful as well because you are not worried about the stock market affecting what you put in your mouth. Remember, for some of you, your needs will be other peoples' wants, it just depends on what lifestyle you want to live.

What is your estimated cost of needs in retirement on a monthly basis? ($_____).

Aim to have that covered from guaranteed income. This is what I prefer for my clients. It is a huge stress relief to know that your basic needs are met no matter what the market does. We will dig into this in part 3.

Dreams: Write down 3 big **dreams** that you have. I want you to really stop and envision what you want these to be. Think about everything that popped into your mind while reading this chapter. Take your time and write them down.

Please fill out all the sections in this section. You will want to refer to these once we start the next part of the book. Having dreams and goals is the most fun part of retirement planning. Your future can be anything that you want it to be, so create that future in your mind and on paper, and let's make that plan a reality!

CHAPTER 3

LIFESTYLE

> "Lifestyle is not an amount; it's a practice."
>
> ~JIM ROHN, AMERICAN ENTREPRENEUR, AUTHOR, AND MOTIVATIONAL SPEAKER

My goal is to create a lifestyle right now that I don't need a vacation from. This involves work that I love, with people I like, doing things I enjoy, living in a place that is conducive to these things, and being around my family. I hear far too many people talk about "needing to get away," which seems like a sad existence to me. If I don't like my lifestyle, it makes more sense to me to change what is necessary to make it perfect for me and my family. This lifestyle shift is a work in progress for me, and I'm sure it will change over time.

When you start to think about the lifestyle that you want to live in retirement, I need you to keep in mind something that is very important. We all have some basic human needs, some of us need all of them, some of us only need a few.

Also, it is important to understand that these needs can change over time. These basic needs are listed below. Keep these things in mind as you are thinking about what you want your lifestyle in retirement to be.

1. **Certainty:** Set schedule, routine, safety.

2. **Variety:** Need to switch things up, get uncomfortable doing the same thing every day. Need to keep moving and doing different things.

3. **Significance:** Have a meaning for your life - Purpose (see previous chapter).

4. **Relationships:** Be around people and have deep meaningful relationships.

5. **Growth:** Grow your experiences and knowledge, and pass things on to the next generation.

6. **Contribution**: A sense of service and focus on helping, giving to, and supporting others. Doing things that make a difference.[1]

I personally love my schedule. If I'm away on vacation, I always feel a little strange when my days are structured differently than usual. You may think it is strange, but I miss work when I'm gone. I thrive on doing mostly the same thing week after week after week, and yes, I do understand that variety is a good thing. Most people, I would say, hate the monotony of their schedule and love to switch things up. I mean, the average person has around 12 jobs in their lifetime. I would certainly call that variety.

So, what do you want your schedule to look like?

- Do you have coffee with friends most mornings?
- Do you still hit the gym every morning?
- Or do you just take life as it comes?

I have multiple clients who have taken their pre-retirement schedules into post retirement. They said they love the structure of that because most of the days are different now, and it is nice to have something that is the same on most days.

In the previous chapter, I hit pretty hard on significance and relationships, and you should understand the importance of those after reading that. Having a schedule and purpose is key to an enjoyable retirement because it gives you a reason to wake up the next day.

Before we move on, I want to dig into growth and contribution. I love the old saying, "if you are not growing you are dying." Yes, I know retirement is a time to slow down and enjoy life, I would argue that you should have been doing that your whole life. But we can't change the past.

Now, maybe you aren't growing yourself anymore (professionally/personally), BUT you can help those behind you grow. Retirees have a vast array of life and career knowledge, to simply retire and never share any of that seems strange, and honestly sad to me.

When you retire, PLEASE share your experiences with those younger generations. Trust me when I tell you the younger generation yearns for you to share your life knowledge and experiences.

I know my wife and I were greatly impacted by a retired couple who led a group Bible study for us at church. We only met 10 times for a little over an hour, but the lessons they taught from their experiences had a profound impact on our faith and family life.

Here is a great example of retirees not sharing their knowledge or mistakes. I have quite a few retirees as clients who say they wished they would have started saving for retirement earlier, and then go on to say how their kids are not saving either. Do you see the problem? Share your regrets and mistakes with younger generations so they don't make the same mistakes.

Here is a great idea for parents, why don't you share with your kids why you wished you would have started to save earlier, and SHARE with them how it would have changed your retirement.

My first two books would also be great resources for them as well. Use your past success and failures to educate those behind you, you will find that impacting others can make you find fulfillment in retirement.

Now that we have a few things in our mind on what some basic needs are, let's imagine what your retired lifestyle looks like. Keep those needs front of mind. Here are some questions to ask yourself to help you determine what your lifestyle looks like.

- Where do we want to live, are we staying put or moving towns?

- Do we downsize our house?

- What do you want to do, and who do you want to do it with?

- Do we move close to kids, or far away from kids?

- What hobbies will we/I be doing?

- What does my schedule look like?

- Do we volunteer more, if so where at?

- Do we travel? Are we snowbirds? Do we have a second home?

- What friends or family do we want to spend more time with?

- Who can we help/impact with our life experiences?

- Do we pick up a new hobby, or adopt a dog to fill up our days?

Your lifestyle is up to you. When you retire, you have the freedom and flexibility to hopefully do what you want when you want. Having an idea of what your lifestyle looks like is going to be critical for you. I don't want you to wake up on day one of your retirement with nothing on your agenda, and nothing in mind that you want to do.

Take some time and think about what your retirement lifestyle will be. Close your eyes, if you must, and imagine it. Are you doing morning walks everyday like I see some retired couples do? Are you solving the world's problems at the local coffee shop every day? Remember to do what makes you happy and consider the basic needs that we all have when you are structuring your retirement.

Something that will help you with determining what this looks like for you is thinking about what your perfect day looks like. Let's use mine to paint an example for you, you will notice some of my needs in this.

Adam's perfect day:

> I wake up early and get a workout in, followed by some time reading or doing a devotional. Have a cup of coffee along with breakfast. Then get the boys fed and take my oldest to school. Then I start work for the day, helping clients with their financial needs. I go home for an early lunch and see my wife and kids, followed by picking up our oldest from school. Then back to work for a while in the afternoon and getting out of the office before 5. The evening is comprised of chasing the kids around/playing outside/going for a walk/or a kid's sporting event and, lastly, eating supper with the family. My wife usually cooks in our home. Once the kids are down, I finally get to sit down with my wife and chat about the day or read before we head to bed, usually exhausted. Then wake up and do it all again!

> *To most of you that may sound like hell, but it's what I truly enjoy. I feel off and anxious if I fall out of this routine. Now, obviously the weekends are different with more family time and church, but I still like to get some work in, and exercise every single day. This is what my perfect day looks like. This doesn't always happen but when it does it is great.*

What does your perfect day in retirement look like? Figure that out and try to repeat it as much as possible. Repeating your perfect day over and over will lead to your ideal lifestyle in retirement.

Top 5 factors to a perfect day for *YOU*.

1. _____

2. _____

3. _____

4. _____

5. _____

CHAPTER 4

PHASED RETIREMENT, PART-TIME WORK

Have you ever run a long race and started out sprinting? I have, and I was absolutely shot about halfway through the race. I mentioned earlier that I was a not-so-successful cross-country runner in my younger years. That's not to say I didn't try some different techniques like starting out sprinting to increase my time. I also tried to wear track spikes, without socks, to make me run a faster race. That just tore all the skin off the back of my feet, leaving me unable to wear shoes for two weeks. I was not an experienced runner at all, and these tricks did not help!

When starting a race, pacing yourself is important. It is the same in retirement. If you start out on a spending spree, you could find yourself broke halfway through your retirement. This is not a situation that is good to be in.

That is why I love the idea of a phased retirement, which means slowly entering retirement. I do want to add I love a phased retirement if you are doing it because you planned for it and want to. It's sad when people are forced to enter phased retirement either because of health or money problems. Being forced to work part time in something that you do not enjoy in retirement is not going to lead to happiness. If you slowly phase into retirement, you can feel your way through it, working in more of what you enjoy, and taking out what you don't enjoy.

A phased retirement allows you to slowly start that retirement race, and most importantly, pace yourself. This will also allow you to work part time and still have purpose and relationships at work, while allowing you more free time to truly get a feel for what your retirement can look like. In addition to those things, the income also helps.

That added income from your part time work can assist your retirement if you retire in a year where we have a down market. However, we do use some distribution strategies that will alleviate most of the risk in retiring in a down market (more on this later). The part time work income can also help if inflation surges 10%, and the cost of everything goes up. We saw this in 2022 with rising food prices, gas prices, and everything else surging.

Having extra income from work allows your investments to continue to grow because you are not taking distributions. The biggest reward of part time work is it mentally allows you to start to see that retirement is possible and it helps you to imagine what your future could look like when you are fully retired.

Part time work is popular amongst retirees. In 2020, over 10 million people aged 65 and older in the U.S. still worked part time, and that number is expected to increase to 16 million by 2030.[2]

Don't feel like you are alone if you are considering this. I do think that continuing to work also keeps you healthily, active, and engaged. For most of you, work was a major part of your life and cutting it out all at once may leave you feeling empty. You have heard the stories of people having all kinds of health issues pop up once they retire. I'm sure some of this is coincidence but having a purpose and something to look forward to is a healthy thing.

One other very important aspect of receiving part time work is it may allow you to delay your Social

Security benefit. Each year you delay taking your benefit you get an increase in the amount that you will receive. This is a lifetime increase!

Delaying your benefit because you do not need it can help you have more guaranteed income in retirement from Social Security. Having more guaranteed income gives you security and allows you to depend less on your investments for income. If you want more security in retirement with higher guaranteed payouts, then you should consider using your part time income to live on and delay your Social Security benefit.

It is easier to keep doing something instead of stopping then starting. Take school for example, for some people, that gap year after high school turns into a lifetime of delaying starting on that degree. The idea of going back to school after you are out and earning an income seems crazy at the time, and not many people are big fans of sitting in a classroom taking on debt instead of earning a living.

If you were to retire straight up at age 62, then the economy tanks along with your investments, and you did not have a proper plan in place then you may be forced to go back to work at age 64/65 to make things work financially. After a year or two off from work you will find it extremely difficult to go back to work.

An easier situation would be to simply go part time at 62 and continue part time for a few years to make sure things work out. I remember some smart man (Sir Isaac Newton – English Mathematician) once said, "An object in motion stays in motion, and an object at rest stays at rest." Take that to heart when you are considering a phased retirement.

Some people do something completely different than what their career was with their part time work in retirement. Don't think that you must stay in the same career field. You could go from a banker to a business consultant, or from a chef to a salesperson. Sometimes a change of pace or scenery will spark your enthusiasm for work again and give you more energy. Your path is yours to blaze.

Dreaming about what you want your retirement to look like should be fun. Retirement is meant to be an exciting time for you. Take time to dream and get a vision of what you want your retirement to look like and **set your goals**.

Now get ready for Part 2 where you will get a wake-up call to see if your goals are possible.

PART 2

WHAT YOU NEED TO DO

> "Saying and doing are two different things."
>
> *AMERICAN PROVERB*

Part 1 was about dreaming about what you want the big picture of your retirement to look like. In Part 2, I want to bring it all together for you. In this part I'll help you determine if your dreams and goals can be met with what you have saved for retirement. Sometimes our dreams don't quite match reality. For example, as a young child I was certain that I would end up in the NBA. I ended up playing a little bit of College Junior Varsity Basketball at a National Association of Intercollegiate Athletics (NAIA) school. Close right?

It's time to talk you through some common retirement investing strategies that are used, and how we like to do things. I'll also give you a guide to Do-It-Yourself if you choose to. I can't stress this enough; everyone's retirement is different. What your plan looks like will differ from your neighbor's based on your needs and wants. Everyone likes things a little different, so what works for one person may not work for another.

The most important part of your own "Redzone Retirement Plan" is executing it. This takes a team and a whole lot of communication. You will see rapid shifts during your retirement in all various areas including taxes, Medicare, stock market swings, interest rates, inflation. If you are not nimble and ready to adjust, you may find yourself in a bad spot fast.

I hope you are reading this book when you are first getting into the Retirement RedZone, which is again five to eight years before retirement. If you make corrections early in the RedZone you can make some significant changes in your plan that could save your retirement. The sooner you plan, the greater difference can be made. If you save a little more, switch up your contribution type, work for an extra year, or pay debt off, it may make a huge difference in your retirement.

Plan early and plan often. If you wait to implement changes the year before your retirement you can do some things that will help. BUT if you make those changes eight years out from retirement those changes can have a bigger impact on your future. Sometimes the smallest tweak in your saving and investing strategy can have a huge impact on your retirement.

I was roommates in college with four football players, and one of them LOVED the movie "Any Given Sunday." That movie has a legendary speech from the coach, played by actor Al Pacino. Part of that speech says this:

> *"You find out life's this game of inches. So is football. Because in either game, life or football, the margin for error is so small — I mean one-half a step too late, or too early, and you don't quite make it. One-half second too slow, too fast, you don't quite catch it. The inches we need are everywhere around us. They're in every break of the game, every minute, every second."*

This quote rings so true for retirement planning as well, small tweaks can make a huge difference. If you don't have a plan in place and you retire in a down market, you may be very unhappy with your retirement. You may be forced to lower your standard of living, or even be forced to go back to work. Tweaking your plan by working a little longer may make all the difference in the world. One error in your retirement plan can have lifelong consequences.

One more thing I need to talk to you about before we start into Part 2 is, **knowing your limits.** I mean we all are not experts in all areas of finance, I even have a team of professionals that I work with daily who know far more about taxes and Social Security than I do. To add to that, far too many of us are irrational and emotional in decision-making. When it comes to making money, emotional decisions are usually not a good idea.

Take casinos for example, they are usually busy and there are a ton of them in the US. We know "the house" always wins, but we still like to gamble and give away our money. My grandpa loved to play Blackjack at the casino. He always said, "Never quit while you are ahead." Not great advice, I know. I'm pretty sure he was joking. Very few people make money in a casino long term, but many people visit them often.

We all have some things that work against us because we make mistakes and are human. In the investing world, these have been heavily researched and are summed up in a field called behavioral finance. The three most common issues from this field that I see affecting retirees are: anchoring, risk aversion, and overconfidence.

Anchoring is an irrational bias towards an arbitrary benchmark figure. This causes you to hold on to a losing stock, because you worked for that company, or you know it will come back. This is dangerous because it skews your decision-making ability. I have found that the more you know, you discover that you don't know that much. This is called the Dunning-Kruger effect. I remember when I first started out as an advisor, and I learned about the 4% Rule. Once I knew that rule, I thought I had retirement planning all figured out, when in fact that knowledge was only the tip of the iceberg. Anchoring is very dangerous and often you don't even see it.

Clothes really aren't my thing. If I had to do my shopping, I would still be wearing clothes from high school. My wife keeps me from anchoring onto an outfit from 15 years ago, which would cause me to look ridiculous. A third party is often the one who can point out your faults, my wife does that for me with my wardrobe. And a good CFP does the same thing for you with your investments and retirement strategy.

Risk Aversion describes the person who prefers a safe investment over the potential for a higher-than-average return. This type of person puts all their money into CDs and money market accounts. If you have more money than you know what to do with, that is fine. For most retirees, leaving money in these safe investments can cause assets to not keep up with inflation. If inflation averages 3% (let alone the 9% we saw in 2022), the cost of everyday life will double every 24 years. If you have a potential for a 30-year retirement, you could face a shortfall in your later years due to the cost of everyday life increasing. Most retirees must have some of their assets that either keep pace with inflation or outperform inflation.

I get it, no one likes to lose, but you cannot let your fear keep you from enjoying your retirement. It's your CFP's job to worry about your plan and make sure everything is working towards your successful retirement. For your investments to keep up with inflation we do have to take on some level of risk. My job is to manage that risk and keep it as low as possible for you.

Overconfidence is the last behavioral finance concept that I want to hit on. This is an ego-driven tendency that leads people to overestimate their understanding of the financial markets and causes them to disregard data and/or expert advice. There is a ton of research that shows the more an individual trades in their account the lower the return versus the market. Overconfidence can lead to large losses in a portfolio, and failure to admit that you were wrong can cause a financial disaster. If you have this problem, it is best to simply use target date funds, managed funds, or hire an advisor. This biggest issue is recognizing this problem, and it is usually pointed out by a third party (advisor).

You won't find me under my car trying to fix it. I don't know nothing about fixing cars, and I'll admit that. Me trying to diagnose my car problem is like the average American trying to create their own retirement plan with no guide. No one likes the person who is overconfident and thinks they know everything. Admitting your shortcomings and asking for help will be a key factor in whether you have a successful retirement plan.

Know your limits and know your tendencies.

Paying attention to these things will help you to avoid some common retirement pitfalls. Get a trusted third party to point out your shortfalls or the holes in your plan. We all have them, figure them out and correct them.

Now, let's dig into part 2. Think of this as your "RedZone Retirement Playbook."

The moves and strategies that you will learn in this final part will help you execute your ideal retirement.

CHAPTER 5

HOW MUCH $ DO I NEED?

> "Success must never be measured
> by how much money you have."
>
> ~ ZIG ZIGLAR, AMERICAN AUTHOR
> AND MOTIVATIONAL SPEAKER

I wanted to start this chapter with how I prefer to do retirement income planning with clients. I prefer to use *The Income for Life Model.* This model uses a strategic combination of Asset Allocation and product selection that has the following goals:

1. Minimize the impact of emotions (Control those things that I talked about in the Introduction)
2. Increase Income to help with the impact of Inflation over time

3. Minimize Risk in the overall portfolio

4. Preserve Principal in the short term, protection from volatility

5. Realize the best possible chance of achieving projected investment results by keeping assets invested over long periods of time.

Below is a description of how this works, and I'll refer to this as we continue through Part 2. The easiest way for me to explain this model is to say that we guarantee that your fixed expense needs are covered by guaranteed sources of income (Social Security, Pensions, Annuities, Reverse Mortgage). We refer to this as your Income Floor.

Next, we make sure that your wants are covered from your other investment sources. And the accounts that we are drawing on today are more conservative than accounts that you will access in the future, which are more aggressive. This model looks different for everyone depending on your feelings toward risk, security, and liquidity concerns. What I love about this model is that it addresses:

Inflation: rising costs in retirement and your income not keeping up

Timing risk: The timing of retiring in a down market can have drastic consequences, this model accounts for that by having the first account that you access invested very conservatively. Also remember, **CASH IS KING**. How much is your goal for cash on hand in retirement? (3-18 months). Having this cash on hand will allow you to withdraw from this account in a down market, allowing your stocks and bonds time to recover.

Longevity risk: Too many people underestimate their retirement timeline. With this model, we can plan on a 30- or more-year retirement to make sure you don't run out of money.

These are the BIG 3 risks that you can face in retirement, and this model solves them perfectly. The Income For Life Model helps us to set up an income floor for you, and it also helps us design the six different buckets of your investments. These buckets are diversified portfolios designed specifically for the level of risk that you are comfortable with, and that you need in your plan for a successful retirement.

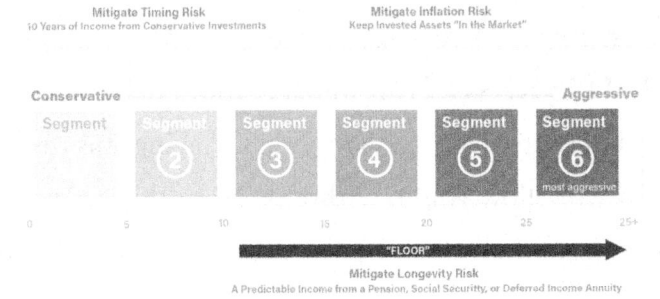

HOW IT WORKS
In one popular approach your deposit is shown as being allocated to six "segments" that will hold invested assets ranging from very conservative to aggressive. Segment one, the most conservative, receives the largest portion of your deposit. Successive segments receive a progressively smaller share of your deposit. The segments receiving the smallest amount of money are those which hold progressively more aggressive assets. The more aggressive an investment, the more risk it is subject to. These segments will be held for the longest period of time in order to achieve the the best possible chance of achieving projected investing results. Allocating your deposit in this manner may help you manage certain risks that could impact the total amount of retirement income that can be generated.

As you move from left to right on the chart's timeline, investments become riskier and are held for longer periods of time in order to boost the potential for higher investment returns. However, there is no guarantee that longer holding periods will reduce risk or increase investment returns.

Determining which investments are appropriate for an individual investor will depend upon the investor's investment objectives and risk tolerance. Please discuss this with your financial advisor before implementing an investment plan. Asset allocation does not guarantee a profit or protect from losses in a declining market. Should the projected rates of return be realized in the various segments, sufficient money will be available to purchase these annuities in amounts capable of providing an increasing level of retirement income. Segment six is shown as a hedge against you living beyond twenty-five years from the date of inception. If that segment meets its projected rate of return, it will hold sufficient assets to continue an income stream. At your death, any remaining assets will pass to your beneficiaries.

If an annuity is selected, guaranteed monthly income is based on current values as well as the terms and conditions of the annuity contract or optional rider. These advantages may have additional fees and can only be fully realized if you follow the benefit's rules and hold the annuity through the surrender period. Cash flow and principal based on the claims paying ability of the issuing company

Copyright 2004-2022 Wealth2k, Inc. All Rights Reserved. The Income for Life Model® is a registered trademark of Wealth2k, Inc.

How much money do you need to retire?

There is no universal answer to this question.

You don't need a certain amount of money to retire, what you do need is a certain amount of **INCOME** from money to retire. You can't take your investment statement to the grocery store to buy groceries, you CAN take your paycheck to the grocery store to buy groceries. What I mean is that it doesn't matter how much money you have, it matters how much **income** you have.

Rules of thumb are very general and should be considered very broad in nature, but they are good tools to use. And here is a general rule of thumb for you. Fidelity estimates that you need 10 times your annual salary by age 67 saved up to retire. So, if you make $100,000 a year you need to have at least $1,000,000 saved by age 67 to be able to retire. Take your household income for that figure if you are married. A secure retirement is all about reliable income, not a specific number on an investment statement. The easy part is saving the money, the HARD part is turning that into income (this is where your CFP comes in). This rule of thumb can be helpful if you're a back-of-the-hand math person.

However, I like to be more specific when we are drilling down into your retirement plan, so keep reading. You hopefully only retire once, so make sure it is right.

Right now, I want you to figure out a few things for your retirement plan. This is for those of you that prefer to do this on your own. If you don't have a CFP or access to the Income for Life software, this is a critical part of the book to pay attention to.

What are your monthly estimated needs per month in retirement $_____

*Think: food, shelter, clothing, insurance, taxes, etc. Refer to your bank statements, and credit cards for estimates.

What are your monthly estimated wants per month in retirement $_____

*Think: vacations, travel, gifts, entertainment, second home, etc.

These numbers should be straightforward for you to figure out. Once you have these numbers down, we are ready to move on to the next step, which is figuring out how we can meet these numbers.

This part may be a sobering moment for you; this is where you find out whether what you have saved will meet your goals. Some may find that you have saved more than enough to meet your goals.

When you are looking at replacing your income another rule of thumb is that you will need between 60-80% of your average gross salary. This is called the *income replacement ratio.* What you do is take your average gross salary for the last three years and multiply that by 60-80%. This will give you a good estimate of how much income you will need in retirement.

Let's give you an easy example. A couple's average gross income for the last three years is $200,000. If they are five years from retirement, they will need around $10,000-$13,300 in monthly income to be able to retire.

You should not need to replace your entire income because you will no longer have to save in retirement, and your taxes should be a little less because of the lower taxation of social security. Again, this is a general rule of thumb, and it does have a 20% variance. Your CFP can help you determine this more accurately.

If you are looking for an all-in-one online calculator, I would suggest you look at: Vanguard, Blackrock, and MarketWatch. They all have free online retirement income calculators for you to use. They will all vary in amounts that they spit out.

Remember what you put in determines what you get out from the calculator, so input the right things. These calculators make quite a few assumptions, so I would use more than one. Then compare them back and forth, usually the answer lies somewhere in the middle.

I will add that your retirement is much more than numbers that you type into a computer, it is an ever-evolving creature. Simple tweaks that they compute could make the biggest difference in the world. That is why I can't stress enough that you have a team of professionals to rely on in retirement.

Figuring out needs and wants is the first critical step in developing your "RedZone Retirement Plan."

The rules of thumb in this chapter should give you a general guide to see if you are on track.

Don't forget the goal of "how much cash do you need on hand in retirement (3-18monts)."

CHAPTER 6

CREATING YOUR DISTRIBUTION STRATEGY

When to retire?

Hopefully, you had a general goal in mind that you wrote down in part 1, use that as your guide right now.

I will add, don't let society tell you what is appropriate, or don't simply retire at 62 because you can draw Social Security. Saving more money in the last five to eight years before you retire can help with the security of your retirement. But working that extra year or working part time for a few extra years can have an even bigger impact. You may have to adjust your plan as your start to work through this part.

Again, this is for people who DIY. If you work with an advisor, this is all done for you behind the scenes.

If you are doing the math in this part and are having a major shortfall, you have a few options: work longer, save more, downsize your retirement.

Let's get started with figuring out the numbers side of things, then we will back into some investing strategies in the next chapter.

This is basic, but it will help you determine how your future is looking. Get the figures from the last chapter right now and copy them below.

What are your monthly estimated needs per month in retirement $_____

What are your monthly estimated wants per month in retirement $_____

Factoring Monthly Needs: $_____*(example $4,000 in Monthly needs)*

Minus (-)

Figure out what your Social Security benefit is at your pre-selected retirement date.

(1)_____*(Example $1,600)*

Minus (-)

Other sources of guaranteed income at that age (pensions, annuity, reverse mortgage).

(2)_____ (*Example $1,800*)

$4,000-$1,600-$1,800= $600 *Example Total:* +$600 *(this is a good thing, the budget has an extra $600 a month)*

Total for you.

(3)_____

Do you have a shortfall?_____ (if you have this, consider alternative options to increasing your income floor: annuities, reverse mortgage, work part time and delay Social Security, etc.) You will need to work with either a broker or advisor to get some of these options on the table. Remember to get multiple options from multiple companies when considering any of the above products.

Now repeat this for your wants.
Monthly Wants:_____
(-) Monthly Income from portfolio_____
=Total_____

To estimate your potential monthly income for your wants: Take your total investable assets times 4%, and then divide by 12.

If you have a shortfall you will need to adjust accordingly.

Again, I like to use *The Income for Life Model* to fund this part of your retirement income needs. The amount of your wants is to be met from the income generated from this system. If you are doing this on your own, try to keep the distribution rate from the total portfolio value around 4%. Set up the six different portfolios based upon your desired level of risk, and you are good to go. (Next chapter we will talk about some portfolio options to consider.)

For example:

Your wants are $3,500 a month, and you have a total portfolio value of $1,000,000. In this example, your distribution rate would be 4.2%. ($42,000 a year in distributions. $1,000,000 / $42,0000 = 4.2%). That rate is a touch high, so when you are first starting out, I would suggest dropping that down by $100-$200 a month.

Additional notes to consider.

4% rule: This is a simple rule of thumb in retirement planning. You simply sum up all your investments and withdraw 4% a year and adjust it annually for inflation.

This is a very general rule of thumb, and it does have one very big issue called "sequence of returns risk." This means that investment returns are unpredictable and can vary year to year. The order of returns on your investments has a huge impact on your retirement plan. If you retire in a down stock market and start the 4% rule blindly, you could greatly enhance the chance that you run out of money. If you are not planning on a long retirement due to health issues, you may bump up your distributions more than 4%. Also, if you are willing to take the risk that you reduce your spending later in life, you may be able to take more than 4% out today. For many people this is a reasonable trade off because they want to be active in their GO-GO years, traveling and having fun. If you are a very conservative investor you may need to dial them back down from 4%.

One simple solution to this is to have enough cash built up on hand to sustain your distributions for 12-18 months. This can be cash in a savings account, cash in a CD, or cash in a life insurance policy. This is a big hole in the 4% rule, and it can be filled by having adequate cash reserves. **CASH IS STILL KING.**

Order of distributions: Where you withdraw from can differ every year based upon your tax situation. It is best to work with your CFP and CPA to develop a strategy to keep you in your desired tax bracket. Remember these change every year, so this is not a set it and forget it strategy, it should be evaluated every year. In general, it is best to take withdrawals from taxable accounts first (brokerage accounts), then from your tax deferred accounts, and lastly spend your tax-free or Roth dollars. In some years you may only take from one, or all three. It all will depend on the amount that you have saved in each, your desired income and tax bracket.

CHAPTER 7

INVESTING STRATEGIES

You should see my wife tie her shoes. She does something very strange with two bunny ears and then pulls them through one over the other. It is confusing and strange to me, but her shoes are tied, and they look the same as mine when I do the: whoop, swoop, and pull. She has me teaching the kids how to tie them the right way – meaning her way. There is more than one way to tie your shoes, and there is certainly more than one way to invest for retirement. In short, everyone does things differently, and what works for you may not work for others. I want to cover a few of the most common types of strategies in the market today.

The following strategies are what you will use to fund the wants part of your plan. This portfolio(s) should be diversified using multiple asset classes (there are 18 available) and designed based upon the level of risk that is appropriate for you. You will find multiple tools online to help you design these portfolios if you choose to DIY (do-it-yourself).

All-in-one portfolio

This first strategy is not one that I like to use, but it is a very common approach to investing in retirement among the DIY crowd. I call this the *"all-in-one portfolio."* This is simply done by putting all your assets into one single portfolio and taking distributions from that on a regular basis only adjusting for inflation every year.

The goal of this stagey is to set up a fixed rate of withdrawals. You design this portfolio based on the level of risk that you want to take. If you use this approach, I highly recommend you have enough cash reserves to cover your expenses for 18-24 months during a down market. Most retirees that do it themselves design this as a 60/40 portfolio. That is 60% stock and 40% bond holdings. If you search online, you will find multiple portfolio-building tools from investment companies like: Fidelity, Vanguard, and Blackrock. If you are doing this on your own, I would highly suggest that you use a pre-built model based upon your desired level of risk.

This all-in-one-portfolio model has been around for years and has some major risks to it. The first risk is sequence of returns risk. That is, if the market has a down year or years, and you continue withdrawals, that could wreak havoc on your portfolio. The other major risk is market risk itself; you have no buffers or features in this account that will prevent losses. Lastly, you run the major risk of moving all this portfolio to cash at the first sight of a market downturn.

Bucking portfolio approach

The second approach is the bucket strategy that I mentioned from "*The Income for Life Model.*" This is where we make multiple portfolios, with each one designed for a specific need for different retirement periods. Bucket #1 is very conservative; this is the money you are spending first in retirement. Buckets 5 and 6 are more aggressive because you won't touch them for 20-25 years. This strategy helps my clients from feeling anxious and wanting to sell in a down market because the portfolios that are affected in a down market have 5 to 10 (or more) years to recover.

I want to close this chapter with some common tools that can be used to cover fixed expenses. Remember, I refer to this as creating your income floor. The floor is created from Social Security and pensions. If you still have a gap between those and your floor, I suggest you look at one of the options below.

Tools to increase your income floor

Annuities: "I hate annuities!" This is part of an actual commercial that one advisor uses. Not all annuities are bad. Saying that is like saying all politicians are corrupt. Okay, maybe that is a bad example, but annuities are a tool, which, if used correctly, can help you live a more secure retirement. Some are good, some are bad if they are not used for the right reasons.

I will add that you never want to put all your money into one contract, which creates a host of issues. I like to use these to build up your income floor if we need to. Or, for buckets in the Income for Life Model depending on your wants and needs. For this book, I'll break annuities into two different types (income and deferred annuities). Make sure you're paying close attention to the fees and restrictions on the product that you buy.

Income Annuities: This type simply provides a monthly payment to you for your life, or if you select a joint life annuity it lasts as long as you and your spouse are alive. If you are concerned about dying early, you can add a death benefit on this contract. One issue with this type of contract is lack of liquidity, so make sure you have adequate assets elsewhere when considering this type of annuity.

Deferred Annuities: This one will give you an income stream in the future. It works the same as the above contract, but the income stream does not start right away. A Qualified Longevity Annuity Contract (QLAC), which I'll discuss more in Part 3, is an example of a deferred annuity.

Freakonomics has a podcast titled "How to Live Longer." In this podcast they say, "People who buy annuities tend to live longer." The basis of the podcast is that people with annuities have less stress about running out of money, and they have an incentive to keep living. That incentive is another paycheck! I like to think of annuities as another form of Social Security, it is a guaranteed lifetime paycheck.

Using an annuity does take market risk off the table for you, and it does set you up with guaranteed income payments. Make sure you are clear about why you want the annuity and what you want to use it for before you purchase it. Also make sure that the company that you purchase it from has a good financial rating and pay attention to fees.

Reverse Mortgage:

This is a mortgage that does not have to be repaid until you and your spouse permanently leave the house. Please don't skip this part because the term "reverse mortgage" freaks you out. These mortgages have become increasingly popular in recent years, and the cost of doing them has also become more affordable. Most times when Mom and Dad pass away, they leave the house to the kids, and what do the kids do? They sell it and simply take the money.

Spoiler alert, most kids have no desire to be in their parents' home.

So, I don't want you to think that your kids will stay in your home when you are gone. I want you to think of your house as an asset that you can use for retirement income. The worst way to use a reverse mortgage is to use it as a last resort in your later years.

You can use this tool in quite a few different ways, it is best used early in your retirement years. You can use it to pay off your current mortgage if you have one. You can also use it as a line of credit, this would be ideal if the market is down, and you have a large expense that comes up. The last most common way to use it is to get a monthly payment for as long as you live in the house. This would increase your income and be a nice tool to increase your income floor.

Don't be close-minded when looking at your income options from your home! This is a great option to consider for increasing income and/or adding liquidity to your retirement. Your home is an ASSET, think of it that way.

To sum this all up:

Steps to creating your "Redzone Retirement Plan."

1. Find your retirement age. _____

2. Set the goal of cash accumulation for that date._____

3. Find the monthly costs of your (Needs) _____ and (Wants)_____ at that age. (Don't forget taxes, health insurance, and any insurance premiums that currently don't have *long-term care options*)

4. Find your guaranteed sources of income at that time. _____. Use this to fund your (Needs). Shortfall?_____

5. *Again, estimate taxes on this part for your SSA benefit, and pensions. If you have a shortfall, consider using an annuity, reverse mortgage, or delaying your Social Security benefit and replacing that Social Security benefit income with part time work or from the portfolio.*

6. Use your portfolio to fund your (Wants) _____.

7. Design these portfolios based upon your desired level of risk. Don't forget taxes, and order of withdrawals. Remember the 4% rule as a rule of thumb. PAY close attention to sequence of returns, and use cash when markets are down. If you have a shortfall on this part, you will need to: save more, work longer, get part time work, or change your wants. If you are doing this yourself, you need to run projections to see how long your portfolio will last every year based upon how you have the money invested and how much you are withdrawing.

8. Evaluate your plan on a quarterly basis to adjust for changes in the market, your life, and the government programs available to you.

CHAPTER 8

LEAVING A LEGACY

> "The idea is not to live forever, but to create something that will."
>
> ~ ANDY WARHOL, AMERICAN VISUAL ARTIST AND FILM DIRECTOR

Questions to ponder:
"What do you want to be said about you at your funeral?"
"What do you want to leave behind for your kids and/or grandkids?"

It is awesome when parents can live the retirement that they want, and still have some assets left over to pass onto the next generation. What I don't like to see is parents pinch pennies in retirement afraid to spend money at all; they put off vacations and buying that sports car. Then when they pass away, all their money goes to the kids and the kids take that fancy vacation and buy the sports car.

In this chapter, I want to talk to you about creating generational wealth, and several strategies that can be used to pass assets onto the next generation so that the money won't get eaten up by taxes. If you are interested in leaving behind assets and want to know more, keep reading about Roth assets, and life insurance - the two powerhouses of generational wealth. If you find that you have some extra funds in your retirement plan, and you want to pass those funds on in the most efficient manner as possible, you should consider these two options.

Roth accounts are one of the greatest wealth accumulation tools because the assets grow tax free, you can take them out tax free, and the next generation inherits them tax free. Roth contributions and Roth conversion are two very powerful ways for you to accumulate Roth dollars. You simply do Roth contributions via your 401k or IRA on an annual basis. Roth conversions are done when you convert pre-tax dollars (IRA or 401K) into a Roth account and pay taxes in the year that you do it.

It is ideal to do a conversion in years where you have a lower income due to the taxation of the conversion. Sometimes it is a good thing for you to pay the taxes so your beneficiaries do not have to worry about giving 30% or more of the inheritance away to the government due to the taxation. This can be a complex transaction depending on the types of accounts that you have so please seek out a professional's help with this. Work with your CFP and Certified Public Accountant (CPA) together to get this done right the first time.

If you have some assets earmarked for beneficiaries, I encourage you to try to get them into a Roth account. Also, I would encourage you to **not be** conservative in how you invest those dollars. We sometimes make this account bucket #6 in the income for life plan. God willing you have a 30-year retirement, if that does happen, we want to make sure that this Roth account designed for the beneficiaries is growing the whole time so that you can use it.

If you pass away and don't use it, at least we got the account some growth along the way by investing it in an aggressive manner. It would not make sense to have this account just sitting gaining nothing for 30 years. Invest this account based on the time horizon and intended use of the account. If this account is meant for someone to get in 30 years or so, and then for them to keep if for another 50 years, you should be investing this money in a diversified stock portfolio.

> "Life Insurance is the only tool that takes pennies and guarantees dollars." ~ Ben Feldman - American businessman and insurance salesman

Based on your age and health, life insurance is an excellent way to leave money behind to beneficiaries as well. The death benefit from life insurance is inherited income tax free, and you can really turn pennies into dollars with this strategy. You can fund this policy with a one-time premium, five, seven, or 10-years' worth of premiums, or a lifetime premium. It is flexible on the design part, and you can pick a benefit that fits your retirement income plan.

Again, say you are done with your plan, and you have enough assets to fund your retirement plus some. And let's say you are not a huge fan of raising your hand to pay taxes on the Roth conversions, then life insurance is an excellent option to consider.

One strategy I like to use if you are in good health is to simply take out .05 - 1% of your portfolio value each year and purchase a life insurance policy with those distributions. This will give your beneficiaries a tax-free benefit. Plus, this policy would have some form of cash value that you could access, if you had to, in the future (worst-case scenario).

Another way to do it is to take out a lump sum from your portfolio and purchase as much life insurance as you can with that amount. Using this strategy, you never have to worry about those premium payments every year in the future. Depending on what type of retirement accounts you have and the taxation of them, this may be a good option to consider.

Life insurance is a powerful tool that can pass on tax-free wealth to the next generation. When used properly, it can leave a legacy that can last for generations at a time. The next question to consider is who we put the life insurance coverage on, husband or wife. That does depend on health, age, and budget. We like to get the biggest bang for our dollar when shopping for these policies for our clients, so we usually get multiple options on the table to consider.

If you are worried about your beneficiaries squandering your inheritance when they receive it, I would suggest you meet with your CFP and attorney to create a strategy to protect and preserve that wealth.

Using either one of these strategies will create the wealth, whether it stays in the family is another issue. A trust can protect these assets for generations if that is a concern of yours. I hate to tell you, but most wealth does not last for more than two generations. Take a family business for example.

> *"Second generation businesses have a 60 percent failure rate, while third generation businesses fail at a rate of 90 percent."*

It is commonly said that the first generation builds it, the second makes or breaks it, and the third generation destroys it. I see this same thing with investments. So, please be prudent in your plan to pass on money and be prudent to protect the money from future generations. Consult with your attorney and CFP to get a protection plan in place.

PART 3

WHAT YOU NEED TO KNOW

> "You don't know what you don't know."
>
> ~ SOCRATES, GREEK PHILOSOPHER

Have you ever done something in your life without looking into it at all, or doing any research on what you were going to do beforehand? I know I have done this more than once. This is how I handle my haircuts most times; I just walk in and say, "Surprise me!"

Sometimes I get a great haircut, other times it's bad. Either way, the only difference between a good haircut and a bad haircut is the two weeks between cuts. I can live with that. Sometimes winging it can have a good outcome, and sometimes it can have a bad outcome. Either way, it's just a haircut. Life is full of positive and negative experiences; I try to have more positives than negatives.

A positive experience that I had in college was when I went on a mission trip to Guatemala with some friends. We really didn't know everything involved with the trip or even what we were going to do when we signed up. There were just a handful of us who thought it sounded like a good idea. We went into the trip blind.

The trip was one of the most positive and life altering experiences that I had in college. The journey and work were awesome, and the experience really changed my worldview in every way. After that trip I looked at every aspect of our American lifestyle in a different way. I began to consider it a luxurious lifestyle compared to those I lived with in Guatemala.

Fast forward a few years, my wife and I signed up for a cooking class on a company trip after a tour guide simply said, "You have to do it, it's amazing." Let me tell you, her idea of amazing and mine are two completely different things. Once again, I had no idea what we were in for, we went into this class blind about what we were going to do. And this class was horrible, we had to cook for four hours. Afterwards the chefs critiqued our cooking for 30 minutes. To top it off, they would not even let me eat the food while I was cooking it. What chef doesn't sample his food while prepping it? (Note to self, don't do a cooking class ever again.)

Retirement can be confusing. You DO NOT want to go into this blind, and hope you get it right. This isn't a two-week fix. Not knowing what your retirement entails can have a lifetime impact. You must be educated about all aspects of retirement if you want to get it right. I don't want your retirement to end up like my cooking class experience, which was a total waste of time. It left me hungry, tired, and upset. If your retirement ends up being unfulfilling, you might not be too happy for a very long time.

*The numbers presented in this part do change annually. To make things simple, I will reference a website for updated numbers. I will also suggest that you work closely with your CPA and CFP to make sure your plan is considering all aspects of the ever-changing tax code.

CHAPTER 9

SOCIAL SECURITY

"Social Security is the very foundation of retirement security for millions of Americans."

~ SUE KELLY, AMERICAN BUSINESSWOMAN AND POLITICIAN

For clarity and emphasis, I'll say it this way: "Social Security is PART OF THE foundation of retirement security for millions of Americans, but it should not be the ONLY thing that you rely on for retirement security."

If you have not set up your online social security management account at SSA.gov I would highly suggest that you do that. The site is a great resource for information we will discuss, and it will show you what your benefit estimates are and show you what your full retirement age is. It is a good idea to review your Social

Security statement before you start your benefits to make sure your earnings are correct.

People ask all the time, "When is the best time to take Social Security?"

My response is usually, "Tell me when you are going to die, and I'll tell you when to claim your benefit."

I'm joking of course. You cannot answer that, but your life expectancy is one of many things that you need to consider when deciding when and how to claim your Social Security benefit.

Here are some others:

1. Sources of guaranteed income: **Pensions**

2. Taxes (gotta love this part).

3. Longevity: How long do you think you will live?

4. Are you married? What is your spouse's benefit? Are you a widow or divorced?

Before we dig into these more, I want you to gain understanding of how Social Security works. Social Security is designed to give you a paycheck, which will increase every year with inflation, for the rest of your life. Here is how this works. If you claim benefits before your Full Retirement Age (FRA), you will get a reduced benefit, AND have a limit on how much earned income you can make.

If you claim after your FRA, you will get an increased benefit, and have no limits on how much income you can earn. In most cases, which increases or decreases you elect is a lifetime decision. If you are still working and do not need the income, we would suggest you delay your benefit until your FRA. However, everyone's situation is different, and you should work with a professional to make the best decision for yourself.

If you are in poor health and longevity is not on your side, then you may consider starting withdrawals early. On the other hand, if you are in excellent health, and everyone in your family lives to 100, then you may be better off delaying your benefit.

If you want to dig deeper into this, I've provided some SSA.gov resources.

What is your Full Retirement Age? *FRA is 66 for people born between 1943 and 1954. But, for people born in the five years after that, the full retirement age again increases in two-month increments each year. See below.*

- *1955: 66 and two months.*
- *1956: 66 and four months.*

- *1957: 66 and six months.*

- *1958: 66 and eight months.*

- *1959: 66 and 10 months.*

- *The full retirement age for Social Security is 67 for everyone born in 1960 or later.*

The reduction for claiming early: *5/9 of one percent for each month before normal retirement age, up to 36 months. If the number of months exceeds 36, then the benefit is further reduced 5/12 of one percent per month.*

So, let's say your Full Retirement age is 66. If you claim benefits at 63, you will take a 20% decrease in your lifetime Social Security benefit.

The increase for delaying: *You'll get an extra 2/3 of 1% for each month you delay after your birthday month, adding up to 8% for each full year you wait until age 70. The clock starts ticking the month you reach full retirement age.*

Again, considering your Full Retirement Age is 66, and you wait until 70 to claim, you would get a 32% increase in your Social Security benefit. You get an eight percent step up in benefit each year you delay your benefit past the Full Retirement age.

Income Limits of claiming early: *If you are under your FRA for the entire year, you would have to deduct $1 from your benefit payments for every $2 you earn above the annual limit. For 2022, that limit is $19,560. This is indexed and changes every year.*

Now let's get back to what you need to consider for yourself in your specific situation. If what you have read so far is really confusing you about Social Security don't worry, this isn't something that you have to figure out on your own. As CFPs, we don't even figure it out on my own when we work with clients. We have software that we use that illustrates different options to clients on when and how they can elect their benefits, and the effect that election has on their benefit amount and potential taxes. The reports from the different software programs makes our recommendations easy and straightforward to our clients related to when they elect their benefit, and how much of their benefit could be included as taxable income.

But I still want you to be able to make an informed decision if you choose to do this on your own. The first thing that you will need to consider are what sources of guaranteed income (remember Social Security, Pensions) you have available to you, and at what age do these income payments start. A few employers still provide pensions to their employees, some of these are great plans, and others not so much. If you have a pension, I suggest doing some research on your own to see how stable the plan is, or have your advisor review the plan. This can be done by examining the annual "summary plan description."

Other sources of income you may want to consider are dividends, interest, and rental revenue. These may or may not be considered guaranteed forms of income, so make sure to analyze their stability.

If you can turn on these sources of income and delay taking your Social Security benefit, you will be able to receive delayed retirement credits and increase your SS benefit. Remember: *if you delay your benefit, you will get an increased benefit for your entire life, or your spouse's life* (in the form of a Widow's benefit). This is a huge benefit that should not be overlooked.

A common error retirees make is tapping into Social Security too early. Your election of when to take Social Security should be part of your "Redzone Retirement Plan." Taking your benefit too early is like a football team kicking a field goal during the first quarter, when it's 1st down at the 10-yard line. This is premature and would be a waste of three downs. Social

Security works the same way, each year you delay, your benefit goes up.

Obviously, you need to compare the pros and cons of which benefit to start first (i.e., consider life expectancy, tax liability, etc.). Make sure that your decision to claim your benefit is part of your overall plan.

Don't forget the potential *taxes* on your benefit. Sorry to burst your bubble but YES, Social Security can still be taxable to you.

Basic Version: The amount of "provisional income" that you make each year dictates how much of your Social Security benefit is taxable.

To determine provisional income, the taxpayer must compute their gross income without Social Security benefits, or the amount of income they collect before drawing Social Security. Then, they should add any tax-free interest they receive from investments, and finally, add one-half of Social Security benefits reported on Form 1099.

Your Social Security benefit can be included at 0%, 50%, or 85% of your taxable income, but fortunately never 100% taxable.

It is not an easy thing to have 0% of your Social Security benefit included as taxable income. **Interesting fact:** It is projected by 2040 that roughly 72% of retirees will file an income tax return. Of those that file, 58% will pay tax on some portion of their Social Security benefit.[3]

If you want to dig into this more, please check out Chapter 13 on Taxes.

Next, you are going want to consider your longevity. If your parents lived into their late 80s or 90s, and you are nearing social security age, you need to take that into account. If you are 62 and perfectly healthy, you may want to wait to claim. However, if you are 62 and have some major health issue, you may want to start your benefit sooner than later.

The breakeven if you wait to claim at 67 versus 62 is 12 years. So, if you waited to take the benefit at age 67 and lived to age 79 you technically made the right choice. (Keep in mind, if you are married and you need a larger widow's benefit for a surviving spouse, it may be best to wait even if you don't have long life expectancy.) Again, if you think that you're going to live past the age of 79 you should wait until your FRA to turn on your benefit.

As mentioned above, if you are married, you also should consider what your spouse's benefit is. One important thing to understand about Social Security is that the surviving spouse gets the higher of the two social security benefits at the first spouse's death. Say the husband has a benefit of $3,000, and his wife's benefit is $2,000. If the husband passes away, his wife will stop receiving her own worker's benefit and start receiving his widow's benefit of $3,000.

One common strategy that is used to protect the ongoing income need of the surviving spouse, is to max out the higher income earner's benefit by waiting to elect benefits after FRA and earning delayed retirement credits to increase his/her benefit.

Here is an example of that: If you are married, one common goal is to optimize the highest benefit that the household has, that is done by waiting until age 70 to take the Social Security benefit.

Say we have Jo and Sally; they are both 66.5 years old and at their FRA. Jo's benefit is $2,500, and Sally's is $1,500. You could wait to take Jo's until 70 allowing it to grow and take Sally's now. If Sally outlives Jo, she will get his higher benefit. This protects the longevity issue that she may face in retirement.

Now, if Jo and Sally were only 60, and Jo passes away, Sally could claim her widow benefit right away and defer her own benefit, allowing it to grow. Generally, widows should elect their benefit as soon as they are eligible.

Lastly, know that if you have a previous marriage that lasted over 10 years you may be eligible for a spousal or widow's benefit from that previous marriage. If that marriage ended in a divorce, and remarriages have happened, you can still be eligible for this. And widow's benefits can begin as early as age 60 versus traditional worker or spousal benefits that can begin at age 62 and 1 month.

In most cases, your decision on when and how to claim your Social Security benefits is a one-time decision, please do not take it lightly. Understand that every person's situation is different, don't simply choose to do as others have done with your personal benefit. Again, SSA.gov is an excellent resource for you to find out more information about Social Security, which can be confusing. This is a critical area that your CFP should be able to help you with.

CHAPTER 10

THE MEDICARE MAZE

Medicare is one of the most confusing parts to retirement, and all the ads on TV and the thousands of mailers that you get in the mail once you are close to age 65 certainly add to the confusion. Never mind the 95 phone calls that you will get per day with companies wanting to sell you coverage. I use the chart below to walk clients through the Medicare maze. It is easy to understand, and it is the best way that I know how to teach you about Medicare.

Medicare was created to provide health insurance coverage, and financial security, for older Americans. Its goal is to ensure health care to elderly and disabled beneficiaries and to prevent them from financial hardship from medical bills.

Medicare Part A	Part A is your Hospital coverage, this also provides some coverage for skilled nursing care.	This coverage is free if you worked at least 10 years, and paid Medicare taxes	Most individuals turning 65 should take Medicare Part A even if you are still employed.
Medicare Part B	Part B covers nonhospital medical expenses e.g.: Doctors' visits, blood tests, X-rays, diabetic supplies…	Part B premiums are based on your MAGI from 2 years ago. And adjust every year. MAGI limits change as well. MAGI: Modified Adjusted Gross Income	Part B should be taken either when you turn 65, or you lose employer benefits after the age of 65.
Medicare Supplements. Cost Plans. Advantage Plans.	Medicare Supplements work with original Medicare and covers costs that Medicare doesn't cover. See below. Plan G is a popular option.	Medicare Cost Plans. Replace Medicare part B. You will still have part A, any facility that accepts Medicare accepts these plans.	Advantage plans replace Medicare and are your primary insurance. Facilities must be in network to accept these. These are referred to as Part C.

102 | REDZONE RETIREMENT PLAN

	Original Medicare: Parts A and B of Medicare are referred to as Original Medicare. This is provided by the federal government provides coverage for doctors' visits, surgeries, and hospital stays for individuals who are enrolled. Parts A and B are taken once you turn 65, or loose employer coverage if you are over the age of 65.		
Drug Insurance Medicare Part D	Helps cover the cost of prescription drugs. These plans may help lower prescription drug costs.	Operated by Medicare approved insurance companies. Research plans at www.medicare.gov	Drug plans can be changed each year during open enrollment October 15th to December 7th.

Medicare Supplements, Cost Plans, Advantage Plans:

Medicare Supplements: Generally, Medicare A/B will cover 80% of your medical bills. A Medicare Supplement Plan G picks up the rest (20%). You do have an annual Medicare Part B deductible, which changes every year. All Medicare Supplement Plan G's offer standardized benefits, however, the prices vary by company. This is the most popular type of Medicare plan that I have historically seen. You will love the coverage that this type of plan provides, but you may not like the premiums that you have to pay. Because of this,

Medicare Cost Plans and Advantage Plans are becoming more and more popular.

Advantage Plans: This will take the place of your original Medicare. You may need to be careful of your network if you get on an Advantage Plan. You will have to make sure that your doctors accept this plan, and if you travel, pay close attention to the out of network benefits. Advantage plans can be an all-in-one solution to your Medicare needs. Some of them include drug coverage, dental benefits, vision benefits, and much more.

Cost Plans: This is a hybrid between a Medicare Supplement and an Advantage Plan. You will still have Medicare Part A, but not Part B. All facilities that accept Medicare will accept this plan. These plans can also include some benefits for: drug, dental, vision, hearing, etc.

Choosing the right plan can be tricky. I always encourage people to consider all options available to them and find the plan that fits their specific needs the best. If you have a ton of medical bills, make sure to get a comprehensive plan. If you never go to the doctor, then you may be able to opt into a plan that shifts more costs on you as the consumer. This will save you in premiums, which means more money in your pocket.

The great news is you can change these plans every year, if you choose to, during the Open Enrollment period. It is best to find a broker who can show you all the options that are available to you. Also, many communities have non-profit organizations that assist you with selecting the best plan for you. You should also research switching your plan every three to five years, if you are healthy, to see if you can save on your premium.

You can sign up for Medicare A and B during your seven-month Initial Enrollment Period. This is three months before your turn 65, the month of, and three months after you turn 65. If you have already started taking your Social Security benefit pre-65, you will be auto enrolled into Parts A and B. You can simply sign up online through SSA.gov or call Social Security at 800-773-1213 to verify.

The annual open enrollment for Medicare is October 15th to December 7th. This is when you can change your coverage if you choose to. If you miss your open enrollment and have a coverage gap, you could face a lifetime penalty if you want to get on Medicare in the future. This is a huge mistake that could cost you money every year the rest of your life, so pay close attention to this so that you get it right.

We can't close out the chapter on Medicare until we talk about the premiums you will have on Medicare. Yes, that's right! You STILL must pay for Medicare Part B, and if you are a high-income earner you may have to pay an additional surcharge for Medicare Parts B and D. This is called the "Income Related Monthly Adjustment Amount (IRMAA)." That is a fancy way of saying you made too much money, so you need to pay more than the standard Medicare premium. Remember, this is a number that looks two years in arrears, and it starts with looking at your Modified Adjusted Gross Income (MAGI) and then adding to that any tax-free bond interest. Adding those two totals will determine your MAGI with respect to IRMAA. So, your Medicare Part B and D premium for 2023 is based on 2021's MAGI.

This IRMAA issue that some people face is yet another reason it is very important to plan for your retirement BEFORE you retire. Income tax planning, and Medicare planning are key in years leading up to your eventual enrollment. Doing some planning for these future costs could save you thousands in your retirement.

Examining this in the real world, in 2023 if you are single and your MAGI from 2021 is **over** $97,000, or if you are married and your MAGI from 2021 is over $194,000 for a joint tax return, you will be subject to the extra surcharge (IRMAA). IRMAA is unique in that it is one of the few taxes that has no "phase-in" with respect to income levels. If you are one dollar above the income threshold tier, you will pay more for your Medicare plan premium.

Again, if you do not sign up on time for Medicare or have a lapse in coverage you may have a late enrollment penalty, so make sure you are paying attention to the dates by which you need to be signed up. Medicare care be tricky, so hopefully this chapter gave you enough information to make an informed decision to select the plan and coverage that best meets your needs. But, as always, I find it best to work with a professional.

Medicare.gov is a great resource for more information on all things Medicare. Many communities have agencies on aging; these are non-profits that can assist you with all things Medicare, and they are great resources to help answer your questions.

CHAPTER 11

LONG-TERM CARE PLANNING

> "No well-planned retirement should be without long term care insurance. It is the very cornerstone of retirement security."
>
> ~ SUZE ORMAN, AUTHOR

Let's define what Long-Term Care (LTC) Planning is. This is the process of planning for your future care if you are no longer able to care for yourself. This care could involve home health care, assisted living care, or even nursing home care. Another part of this process is deciding how you are going to pay for this care. Are you paying cash for the care, or is insurance going to pay for this care?

This MUST be part of your Retirement RedZone Plan, failure to plan for this could result in financial ruin. You not having a plan for your LTC needs would be like a football team not having a quarterback on the roster. And yes, it is that important!

I'd like to start this chapter with some stats for you about LTC.

- If you live to age 65 you have a nearly 70% chance of requiring long-term care services in the future. [4]
- Average stays in a long-term care facility: Women (3.7 years), Men (2.2 years).
- Average cost is $5,000-$9,000 a month, depending on type of care.[5]

The cost of long-term care (if you need it) could cripple any retirement plan if it is not properly planned for. Many planners fail to mention or talk about long term care costs because of the complexity of the conversation, lack of knowledge about insurance options, and the inability to have solutions to solve this problem.

Talking about or even thinking about ending up in a nursing home, let alone going into one, is not a fun conversation to have. Each of my grandparents, and many of my clients, have been in a facility at one time or another, so I feel I can speak about this topic with a high degree of empathy and knowledge.

Many people (usually men) when approached with this conversation have common responses.

1. I'll never go into a nursing home. I'll take myself out long before that happens and solve that problem myself.

2. I'll have the government pay for it.

3. My kids will take care of me.

4. That will never happen to me.

5. It's too expensive.

These responses are an immature cop out to keep from addressing the problem at hand. We all get old, and facing our declining future is not a fun topic to consider, and a lot of times it is easier not to think about it at all. But if I'm doing your future retirement justice, I cannot allow you to simply skip out on one of the most important planning aspects of your retirement. You must have a plan in place to pay for this potential care. If you don't properly plan for your care, you could leave your surviving spouse pinching pennies to make ends meet. And if you think long term care insurance is expensive, try not having it!

Don't think of long-term care insurance as nursing home insurance, think of it as stay-at-home insurance. Policies allow you to receive care right in your home, so you don't have to go into a facility.

Hopefully, you now understand the importance of planning for your long-term care needs, so let's get into some of the most common ways of protecting your retirement from the nursing home. You could have the most complex and perfect investment strategy in the world, but it will not save your retirement from an added expense of $9,000 a month.

> "We insure against what can go wrong in order to acquire the luxury to invest for what can go right."
> ~ Nick Murray, Author

Insurance is the most common way to protect yourself against the cost of long-term care.

The two most popular types are: Traditional Long-Term Care, and a newer Hybrid Life Insurance/Long-Term Care combo product. Highlights of each follow, but you should work with your planner to find the best product to fit your specific needs.

Traditional Long-Term Care

Historically this is the most common type of coverage. This product pays for: Home Health Care, Assisted Living, Nursing Home, Adult Day Care, etc. The premiums for this can be tax deductible up to certain limits if you are self-employed or own a business. These policies have a use-it or lose-it benefit. Meaning if you don't need to use the policy and you pass away, all the premiums you paid are lost. Also, the companies that provide these policies do reserve the right to increase the premium on existing policies in future years.

To qualify for LTC policy benefits you need to need help with at least two of the six activities of daily living: walking, eating, bathing, dressing, transferring, and continence. Some states also have long term care partnership programs, this is dollar-for-dollar protection from Medicaid. Every dollar that a qualified long term care policy pays out on your behalf is an extra dollar of protection that you get from the Medicaid spend down limit. This "Partnership Program" offers asset protection (protection of savings from the asset limit and protection from estate recovery of the home) to Medicaid applicants. To be clear, this program protects assets, not a Medicaid applicant's income. (More on this later.)

Life Insurance/Long-Term Care Hybrid policies

These are honestly my favorite type of coverage options. These are life insurance policies with a LTC rider built in that allows you to accelerate the death benefit for your own long term care needs. So, no matter if you end up in a nursing home or pass away prematurely, someone is going to be the beneficiary of your life insurance policy. Either you personally, or your beneficiaries.

Example: Joe has a $500,000 life insurance policy with a Long-Term Care rider on it. Joe ends up in the nursing home for three years, and it costs $100,000 a year. Joe passes away after using $300,000 for LTC, the remaining $200,000 will go to his beneficiaries. All income tax free. These are more expensive than traditional long-term care policies because you also have the life insurance protection for your family.

I always like to stack these options side-by-side for clients to look at. Depending on the situation, we will use one or the other, or sometimes it is a combination of the two. A huge problem is usually people are not healthy enough to qualify for insurance, because they wait until they are 65 or over to consider these. If you ask Dave Ramsey, he will say to get LTC insurance at age 60, but Suze Orman has changed her tune after her mother didn't qualify and now says consider purchasing LTC insurance at age 50. I always tell clients, **"Get it the day before you need it."** (Joking of course.)

So, what is the perfect age to get it?

With the hybrid combo product (via the LTC rider) it does make it inexpensive to obtain coverage in your 40s and 50s. However, I don't know of too many 40-year-olds who are concerned about living in a nursing home. Again, everyone's situation is different, but **I would highly suggest you start to seriously consider LTC insurance once you hit age 50. And of course, better late than never.** The best part of this combo product is that the cost of insurance never increases with the LTC rider.

The cost of these policies can vary based upon your health and amount of coverage that you desire. I prefer clients get a middle of the road policy that will cover them for three to four years and pick up 90+% of the projected future cost. It is not the extra $500 a month that will break most retirement plans, it's the extra $5,000 a month. I always look at insurance with a "minimum effective dose" kind of viewpoint. So, please get a policy in place that will cover at least your basic daily living needs if you need care.

There are also asset based long-term care coverage options. With these contracts, you give an insurance company a large sum of money (example $100,000), and if you go on claim (into a nursing home) they will double or triple your money ($200,000 or $300,000). Asset based long-term care contracts are extremely situational when they are appropriately used and as a client you need to have a large pile of cash to make these work.

Medicaid:

You should not rely on Medicaid to foot the bill for your long-term care needs. The asset spend-down, and income limits for Medicaid are very low. Consider these roughly estimated numbers (these figures do change every year).

Don and Nancy are married, they have a total of $1,500,000 in liquid assets, a $500,000 home, and three cars. Don enters a nursing home, and the monthly cost is $8,000. Don and Nancy will have to private pay for his nursing home stay until **they have under $130,000 in liquid assets, one house, and one car. At this point Medicaid will kick in and start to pay for Don.** *(Each state has its own eligibility and spend down requirements, as well as provisions to consider for the community or well-spouse income limits.)*

Now, you may be wondering why they don't opt to get rid of all their money when or before Don goes into the nursing home, that way they protect their money. Well, don't worry! Our government is a step ahead of you on that one. If you transfer assets below market value or gift money within five years of applying for

Medicaid, the government reserves the right to count those assets toward the application for eligibility.

Medicaid is not a great option mainly because it can result in the healthy surviving spouse being impoverished. I have seen significant sums of money lost to the Medicaid spend down. When you hear of family "losing the farm to the nursing home," this is exactly what they are talking about. If you are in this situation, I would highly suggest working with a Medicaid or Elder Care attorney.

With proper planning, an Irrevocable Trust can also be a tool to protect assets from Medicaid.

Putting your assets into this trust effectively removes your ownership rights to the assets. You will name one or more beneficiaries to the trust. You cannot make changes following its creation and funding. You will not be able to modify, amend, or terminate this type of trust without the use of a trust protector. With proper planning, you will not need to worry about Medicaid counting the assets in the trust against you. This can be used as part of your planning strategy for your long-term care needs. I suggest that you work with an estate planning attorney if this is a strategy that you are considering.

If you don't plan for the increased cost of long-term care for your retirement, you may be shocked when a care need arises. Put a plan in place to take care of this potential pitfall. To close, if you have under $150,000 in retirement assets, long-term care insurance probably is not for you. If you have over $8,000,000 in retirement assets it is not for you. In my opinion, it is middle America who needs to plan and protect their retirement with a LTC strategy.

CHAPTER 12

ESTATE PLANNING

> To put Estate Planning simply, it is,
>
> "Organizing what you have, protecting it, and making sure it goes where you want it to go when you die."

End of chapter...

I wish it were that easy, trust me, but we need to dig in a little more. This chapter will walk you through several estate planning essentials, so you have a basic understanding of what you will need to have, to think about, and to do. Creating an estate plan means working with an attorney who specializes in estate planning, I would not suggest doing it online. Your CFP should be able to give you a referral, or if you are going to research attorneys on your own then interview several and select the one that best fits your needs.

The most important part of estate planning is letting your beneficiaries know what your desires are and why. Far too many times family fights and arguments about who gets what are had after Mom and Dad are gone. If the patriarchs in the family would have sat everyone down together and explained to them what they wanted to happen with their assets and why, many fights and arguments could be avoided. If you have assets and multiple kids don't wait until after you are gone for them to figure out what happens, communicate your desires before you pass and justify why you want these things to happen.

The next most common error that I see is not having up to date beneficiaries on investments, qualified plan assets, insurance contracts, and bank accounts. If you name a beneficiary on your investment and insurance accounts, those assets will pass directly to the beneficiary. You can set more than one beneficiary and you can give the exact percentage that you want for each beneficiary. If you are comfortable with these beneficiaries getting access to this money right away with no limits, doing this makes things flow smoothly. You should also set up a TOD (Transfer on Death) designation on your: bank accounts (these may also be listed as POD, Payable on Death), CDs, and brokerage accounts. This will allow this account to directly transfer to your beneficiary, simply contact the bank or custodian to make this change. Doing these simple things will help these assets pass to heirs directly without going through probate. Probate is the process of the court verifying the assets, paying off debts of the estate, and then distributing remaining assets, if any. This is more expensive and takes longer.

Documents to have in place:

The first document you want professionally drafted according to your state is a will. A will is a playbook for the distribution of your assets. Every adult should have a will in place. This document spells out where all the assets go, and how they are to be distributed. A will allows you to control the distribution of your assets from the grave. If you die without a will, it's called dying intestate, and instead of you deciding who receives your assets, the courts will determine where your things go. That can potentially be expensive, because usually family members are going to fight over who gets what. In addition to a will, you should also designate a financial and medical power of attorney, as well as draft a living will. These things give authorization to others to take care of things for you if you are unable to speak for yourself. I would suggest you also explain to the whole family why and who you selected as power of attorney to avoid potential fights/arguments in the future about who gets to make what decisions for mom and dad.

Trusts

Trusts can be used to provide legal protection for assets, and also designate over time how to distribute assets. They can also help avoid or reduce inheritance or estate taxes. The Estate Tax limit is ever changing in our country, and if you are above the estate tax limit, trusts can be a tool to keep more of your assets in your family and less going to pay the federal or state estate tax. The 40% federal estate tax is steep, and if you have significant assets, your estate can be severely reduced if you do not properly plan. Since 2010, the estate tax exemption amount has varied from $5,000,000 to a little over $12,000,000. Trusts can be complex; it is very important that you work with an estate planning attorney to develop a specific strategy for you. If you have assets within these historical limits, it is of utmost importance that you meet with an estate planning attorney as part of your RedZone Retirement Plan.

Leaving a Legacy

Once you have your retirement income plan in place, the natural next step is to consider legacy planning for loved ones. Some people may not consider how transferring these assets that work well in retirement could negatively impact a beneficiary when the asset transfers to them at death. IRA distributions are income taxable to beneficiaries, while Roth distributions are tax free, and stocks in a brokerage account, land, or other physical assets provide beneficiaries a step-up in basis. This can change if our tax environment changes, but it is something that I want to point out. Say you buy a stock for $1, hold it for 30 years, and pass away when it is worth $10. If your beneficiary inherits that stock and sells it at $10, they have no tax liability due, this is called a step-up in basis. This goes for long term assets, like land and physical assets as well.

I say this to make you aware of how you are dividing assets. Let's say you have two kids, Jon and Jenny, and you have $1,000,000 in an IRA, $500,000 in a Roth, and $500,000 in land. It is not equal to just give the IRA to Jon, and the rest to Jenny. You need to pay attention to the taxation of the assets when you pass if you want all things to be equal. In this situation the

IRA would be 100% taxable to Jon, and Jenny could get all tax-free assets.

It is popular for clients to leave life insurance as a legacy tool and as an estate planning tool. Life insurance passes income tax free to the beneficiaries. It can also be used to pay estate taxes on a large estate, so that assets do not have to be sold to pay the tax liability. Or it can simply be used to give the beneficiaries a tax-free inheritance and help an executor take care of any estate settlement costs.

Here is an example: Bill and Marge are each 65, both retired, and have $1,000,000 in a taxable IRA, along with Social Security and a pension. They live a comfortable lifestyle, and they want to guarantee that each of their two kids get $200,000 when they pass. A simple tool is for Bill and Marge to get $400,000 total of life insurance coverage by each of them purchasing $200,000 permanent coverage. And to pay the premium, they take a little bit from their taxable investment account each year and leverage those taxable dollars to have a larger tax-free asset for their children. This way, even if the investment account is worth $50,000 when they die, the kids still each get $200,000. Plus, the life insurance is income tax free.

In closing, estate planning is a very important thing to get in place while you still can make informed decisions. Work with an attorney to get your plan in place, and make sure your CFP is involved in the conversation. Most importantly COMMUNICATE with all your beneficiaries about all aspects of your plan, what you want done, and why. It is much better coming from you while you are still here.

Unless an exception applies:

If you take a distribution of Roth IRA earnings before you reach age 59½ and before the account is five years old, the earnings may be subject to taxes and penalties. Withdrawals of earnings and deductible contributions in a traditional IRA before you reach age 59½ are subject to ordinary income tax and penalties. An early withdrawal from a traditional 401(k) will be taxed as regular income and subject to penalties.

CHAPTER 13

TAXES

> "...but, in this world, nothing is certain except death and taxes."
>
> ~BENJAMIN FRANKLIN, FOUNDING FATHER OF THE UNITED STATES

Taxes are already confusing, and to make it even more difficult the laws change every year. In fact, **the current IRS tax code has more words in it than the Bible does.** A common thing for Christians to do is to try to read the Bible in an entire year, if you have done this, I doubt that you remember every word and story from that entire year. The Bible does not change at all, ever.

On the other side, the IRS code has changed every single year. Good luck keeping up with all of that. Maybe that is why most CPAs and accountants are always upset/cranky/quiet/busy/etc. I would be too if the rules that I must play by changed every year. I'm just joking, Mom! (My mom is a CPA).

Social Security, Medicare, dividends, capital gains, income, and estate taxes are confusing, and we all hate paying them. This chapter will walk you through the fundamentals of these taxes and what you need to understand. You need to have a simple understanding of these taxes and how they work in retirement so that you can make informed retirement distributions when it is time.

I'll also end the chapter talking about Required Minimum Distributions (RMDs). These numbers do change from year to year, and the tax code can change as well. For the most up to date information, please check out IRS.gov or consult with your CPA or CFP. Some things in the chapter may make your head spin. But please stay focused because this is very important.

Where you take distributions from, along with how much, can play a HUGE role in the amount of taxes you owe. Some believe the general order of distributions is: Take from taxable accounts first (take advantage of lower capital gains tax, and dividend tax), next take from your tax-free accounts (Roth), and lastly take distributions from your traditional IRAs and 401k.

Doing this is like saying that a football team should ALWAYS run on first down, pass on second down, and run on third down. It doesn't work like that during a game, and it doesn't work like that in your retirement.

There is a better way to do your distribution planning. Do it every year, while doing annual income tax planning, and Retirement Minimum Distribution (RMD) planning, which we will discuss later in the book. It is highly likely that your distribution strategy will be different every year. It is rare that my clients follow the general order of distributions, because every client is unique, and the ever-changing tax code makes tax planning a critical part of your RedZone Retirement Plan.

Social Security

To determine what amount of your Social Security benefit will be included as part of your taxable income (0%, 50%, or 85%), you first need to calculate your provisional income. Your provisional income is generally equal to the combined total of (1) half of your Social Security benefits, (2) your tax-exempt interest, and (3) your adjusted gross income (minus certain deductions and exclusions).

Once you have that figured out, simply use the chart below to determine what percent of your Social Security benefit will be considered taxable income. This may change from year to year. I will add that it is very difficult to get into the 0% tax, it is something you can try, but if you have a pension, or high RMDs it may be impossible.

Social security also has an online calculator you can use.[6]

Social Security Taxation Threshold Table

Single	Married, filing jointly	% of benefits are taxable
$0 - $25,000	$0 - $32,000	0%
between $25,000 and $34,000	between $32,000 and $44,000	50%
more than $34,00	more than $44,00	85%

This is a great website to see how this works and to see the updated annual numbers on the income tax limitations on Social Security.[7]

If you start your benefits before your full retirement age, you may have part of your benefits withheld and paid out at full retirement age, if you earn more than the annual earnings limit. *If you are under full retirement age for the entire year, you will get $1 deducted from your benefit for every $2 you earn above the annual limit.* **For 2023, that limit is $21,240.**

In the year you reach full retirement age, you get $1 deducted in benefits for every $3 you earn above a different limit. **In 2023, this limit on your earnings is $56,520.** Only your earnings up to the month before you reach your full *retirement age is counted, not your earnings for the entire year. IF you are starting your Social Security benefits before your full retirement age, you must watch how much earned income you are making.*[8]

Medicare

This isn't necessarily a tax, but it is a surcharge added to your Medicare premium if you are a high-income earner. In my mind, that is like a tax, maybe they thought IRMAA (Income Related Monthly Adjustment Amount), which we talked about earlier, sounded better than tax or penalty when this was created. I think of this like all the healthy snacks that we have now, sugar is sugar, and a tax is a tax. Okay, let's get back to it.

This was briefly covered in the Medicare chapter, but here is a quick recap for you. Income Related Monthly Adjustment Amount (IRMAA) is a fancy way of saying you made too much money, so you need to pay more for your Medicare coverage. This is a number that looks two years in arrears, and it is based on your Modified Adjusted Gross Income, which we referred as MAGI earlier, Adjusted Gross Income (AGI) plus any tax-free bond interest. Your Medicare Part B and D premium for 2023 is based on 2021's MAGI. Below are the full charts for you.[9]

Medicare Part B IRMAA premiums.

Full Part B Coverage

Beneficiaries who file individual tax returns with modified adjusted gross income:	Beneficiaries who file joint tax returns with modified adjusted gross income:	Income-Related Monthly Adjustment Amount	Total Monthly Premium Amount
Less than or equal to $97,000	Less than or equal to $194,000	$0.00	$164.90
Greater than $97,000 and less than or equal to $123,000	Greater than $194,000 and less than or equal to $246,000	$65.90	$230.80
Greater than $123,000 and less than or equal to $153,000	Greater than $246,000 and less than or equal to $306,000	$164.80	$329.70
Greater than $153,000 and less than or equal to $183,000	Greater than $306,000 and less than or equal to $366,000	$263.70	$428.60
Greater than $183,000 and less than $500,000	Greater than $366,000 and less than $750,000	$362.60	$527.50
Greater than or equal to $500,000	Greater than or equal to $750,000	$395.60	$560.50

Medicare Part D IRMAA premiums.10

If your filing status and yearly income in 2021 was

File individual tax return	File joint tax return	File married & separate tax return	You pay each month (in 2023)
$97,000 or less	$194.000 or less	$97.000 or less	your plan premium
above $97,000 up to $123.000	above $194,000 up to $246,000	not applicable	$12.20 + your plan premi'um
above $123,000 up to $153,000	above $246,000 up to $306,000	not applicable	$31.50 + your plan premi'um
above $153,000 up to $183,000	above $306,000 up to $366,000	not applicable	$50.70 + your plan premi'um
above $183,000 and less than $500,000	above $366,000 and less than $750,000	above $97,000 and less than $403,000	$70.00 + your plan premi'um
$500,000 or above	$750,000 or above	$403,000 or above	$76.40 + your plan premi'um

This IRMAA premium can have a major impact on your annual cost of Medicare. Just look at those charts above again. This is something that we pay close attention to when doing retirement distributions for clients each year. You need to evaluate the annual income limits for IRMAA and try to keep your Modified Adjusted Gross Income in the desired bracket.

Remember, this does not catch up to you for two years. I have had clients change the type of distributions that they are doing (taxable versus tax free), or even stay on an employer plan if it is still available due to these IRMAA penalties.

Dividend and Capital Gain

In a perfect world, you would have all tax free (Roth) income in retirement, which would be a safe way to avoid some of these taxes in retirement. Well, we don't live in a perfect world, or a safe world. I'm sure you are aware of that. I can't even ride a bike without a helmet anymore without getting scolded. I rode my bike 10,000 miles as a kid, and we never even knew what a helmet was. Drivers are constantly on their phones, and the runners don't like you on the sidewalk. The world is never going to be perfect or safe, but me riding my bike with a helmet may make it safer. Dividends and long-term capital gains (if you are over the 0% bucket) are not tax free, but they are taxed at a lower rate than your pre-tax traditional IRA's and 401k. If you receive dividends and long-term capital gains inside of your IRA or 401k, this does not apply. The tax status of your IRA is the default taxing method on those accounts. All dividends and capital gains inside a traditional IRA/401k are taxable, all dividends and capital gains in a ROTH account are tax free.

Dividends are taxed in a few different ways if they are held in a taxable account: Qualified and Non-Qualified. If the dividends don't meet the qualified criteria, they are simply taxed as non-qualified dividends. In short, you want your dividends to be qualified.

Qualified dividends are taxed at 0%, 15%, or 20%, depending on your income level and tax filing status. To meet this requirement, the dividends must be either listed on a major stock exchange or based in the USA. And you must hold them for a 121-day period. The 121-day period begins 60 days before the next dividend is distributed. This mandatory holding period prevents stock traders from earning tax-advantaged income on stocks that they hold for only a few days. See the chart below for details.

Ordinary (non-qualified) dividends and taxable distributions are taxed at your marginal income tax rate, which is determined by your taxable earnings.[11]

2023 Ordinary Dividend Tax Rate	For Single Taxpayers	For Married Couples Filing Jointly	For Heads Of Household
10%	Up to $11,000	Up to $22,000	Up to $15,700

12%	$11,000 to $44,725	$22,000 to $89,450	$15,700 to $59,850
22%	$44,725 to $95,375	$89,450 to $190,750	$59,850 to $95,350
24%	$95,375 to $182,100	$190,750 to $364,200	$95,350 to $182,100
32%	$182,100 to $231,250	$364,200 to $462,500	$182,100 to $231,250
35%	$231,250 to $578,125	$462,500 to $693,750	$231,250 to $578,100
37%	Over $578,125	Over $693,750	Over $578,100

Capital Gains: Long Term and Short Term

Capital gains taxes are due on the profits earned from the sale of assets. Some examples might be stocks, real estate, businesses, and other types of investments in non-tax-advantaged accounts (think about your taxable brokerage account).

To simply put it, the capital gains tax is calculated by taking the total sale price of an asset and deducting the original cost. If you hold the asset for over one year, that is a long-term capital gain. If you hold it for under one year, that is a short-term gain, and it will be taxed as ordinary income. You always want to try to get assets taxed as long-term capital gains; these taxes can be either 0%, 15%, or 20%. The percentage you pay is based on your total taxable income. Below are the tables for 2023, again these will change every year.[12]

2023 Long-Term Capital Gains Tax Rate Income Thresholds

Capital Gains Tax Rate	Taxable Income (Single)	Taxable Income (Married Filing Separate)	Taxable Income (Head of Household)
0%	Up to $44,625	Up to $44,625	Up to $59,750
15%	$44,626 to 492,300	$44,626 to $276,900	$59,751 to $523,050
20%	Over $492,300	Over $276,900	Over $523,050

Here is an example for you: You bought an individual stock worth $50 on January 15th, then that stock went through the moon, and you sold it on March 12th for $500. You made a nice profit of $450. Not bad right? Well, in this scenario, you sold it within the first year so that profit is taxed as ordinary income. What if you would have waited one year to sell that stock, it would have been taxed as a long-term capital gain, which could be a lower tax rate for you. This same thing goes for any real estate or business that you buy and sell as well.

Pay careful attention to the taxation of your assets if you are buying and selling them on a frequent basis.

Income Taxes

I'm sure you are sick of looking at numbers and thinking about taxes by now. Stick with me, we just have a few more things to get through.

Don't forget that you have federal and state income taxes that will be due in retirement as well. These taxes are based on the amount of income that you earn, and what state you live in. Some states are more favorable to retirees' income taxes than others. What state you live in during your retirement can play a major role on how much you pay in taxes. Below is a great chart that shows some of the friendliest tax states for retirees and other not so friendly states. Again, these taxes can change every single year, so this list will change over time.[13]

For example, Nebraska, where I live, is only one of 12 states that still taxes your social security benefit on a state income tax level. Nebraska has passed legislation that will completely phase out the taxation of social security by the year 2030.

Very Tax Friendly	Tax Friendly	Moderately Tax Friendly	Not Tax Friendly
States that either have no state income tax, no tax or retirement income. In addition, states in this category have friendly sales, property, estate and inheritance tax rates.	States that do not tax Social Security income and offer an additional deduction on some or all other forms of retirement income. Generally, states in this category also have relatively friendly sales, property, estate, inheritance and income tax rates.	States that offer smaller deductions on some or all forms of retirement income. The sales, property, estate, inheritance and income tax rates in this category range in friendliness based on the degree of retirement deductions available.	States that offer minimal to no retirement income tax benefits. These states also do not have particularly friendly sales, property, estate and inheritance tax rates.
Alaska Florida Georgia Mississippi Nevada South Dakota Wyoming	Alabama Arkansas Colorado Delaware Idaho Illinois Kentucky Lousiana Michigan New Hampshire Oklahoma Pennsylvania South Carolina Tennessee	Arizona District of Columbia Hawaii Indiana Iowa Kansas Maryland Massachusetts Missouri Montana New Jersey New Mexico New York North Carolina	California Connecticut Maine Minnesota Nebraska Rhode Island Vermont

The limits on income taxes change every single year as well, so make sure you are updating your plan annually based upon the changing tax code. I prefer to collaborate with a CPA when I'm helping clients make these important tax decisions.

Estate Taxes & Inheritance Taxes

You have just read about most of the taxes that you will have to pay while you are alive. In addition to that, your estate can also possibly be taxed when you pass away as well. I know, for some of you the taxation does not ever stop. The good news is the estate tax exemption amount is pretty high on the federal side, and the inheritance tax and estate tax on the state level is not imposed by all states. When it is imposed, it ranges from 0-20%. These taxes do not apply if the assets pass to a spouse, this only applies when they go to the next generation or outside family members.

Estate taxes are due at the federal level when you pass away and have assets over a certain value and pass those assets onto the next generation. This tax is at 40% in 2023, this can vary based upon current tax code. Since 2010, the estate tax exemption amount has varied from $5,000,000 to a little over $12,000,000. The most common people that are subject to this tax are individuals with businesses or hard assets (land, rental property, business property). If you have a family business, this estate tax can potentially destroy the business because of the taxes owed at death of the primary owner. If the business does not have enough cash, some of the business assets may have to be sold to pay the federal estate tax. This could cause major issues in the operation if almost half of it must be liquidated. Below is an example.

Jo and Suzie are farmers, they inherited family farm ground from both of their parents, and both of their sons work on the farm. They have farm ground, equipment, and retirement accounts with a total value of $13,000,000. Jon and Suzie both pass away in a car accident, and they each have an estate tax exemption amount of $5,000,000, so $10,000,000 total. Their boys could potentially have an estate tax due of $1,200,000. ($13,000,000 estate - $10,000,000 exemption amount = $3,000,000 x 40% = $1,200,000), plus any state estate taxes due, or state inheritance tax. If the estate does not have $1,200,000 in cash, the boys may have to liquidate some assets to pay the taxes. A common simple solution for this could have been, Jo and Suzie buy a second-to-die life insurance policy in an irrevocable trust for $1,500,000. This type of policy pays on the last death (whether it is Jo or Suzie). This way the contract payout can be used to pay the estate tax and keep the whole farming operation in the family.

The state inheritance tax and estate tax can vary from state to state and not all states have it. Eleven states and Washington D.C. have a potential state estate tax, and six have an inheritance tax. Hawaii and Washington have the highest estate tax at 20%. Nebraska has the highest potential inheritance tax at 18%. These taxes also can have exemption limits and do depend on your relation to the deceased. Working with an estate planning attorney can help you legally avoid some of these taxes through the tools and strategies that they use.

Required Minimum Distributions (RMDs)

Let's have a short conversation on Required Minimum Distributions (RMDs), which I briefly mentioned earlier. These currently start at age 72. With the way the tax code reads right now, you must either take it by 12-31 weeks in the year you turn 72, or by April 1st of the following year. If you wait and take it the following year, keep in mind you will have two RMDs in one year, which may put you in a higher income tax bracket. RMDs are required on all pre-tax accounts (IRA's, 401k, 403b, etc.) that you have. The percentage you must take out is 3.7% when you turn 72, and it goes up from there as you age. Let's say you have a total of $1,000,000 in your pre-tax accounts. At age 72 you would have to take out $37,000 that first year as an RMD.

It doesn't matter if you retire at age 60 or 70. If you are not looking into the future and calculating what your RMDs will be and how it will affect your taxes, you are not doing proper retirement planning. Working with your CFP and CPA you should be able to structure a proper distribution strategy that accounts for your future RMDs.

Okay, we are done talking about taxes for now. As you can see, this is a very complex part of retirement planning. If you are a DIY planner, make sure you understand these concepts and update your plan on an annual basis to account for these things. If you are working with a CFP, make sure they have a connection with your CPA and are working together on the best strategy for you. Some of the consequences of having too much income won't catch up to you for two years. This may leave you feeling like I felt when the coach was chewing me out for not "shooting the A gap." He accepted my answer of, "I didn't know." Unfortunately, the IRS will not accept that answer.

This concludes our last section - What you need to know.

This has given you a base level understanding of some of the ins and outs of retirement planning. It is important, whether you are doing this yourself or working with a planner, that you understand these things. This last part is the most complex part of the book, but as important as the first two parts. The tax code changes every year, and it is essential that you stay up to date on these changes. You don't know what you don't know, and ignorance is not going to serve you well in retirement. In my first few years in business, I had no idea about 80% of what you just read.

In my second year in business, I suggested that a client drop his group health insurance to get on Medicare and a Medicare supplement. At that time, I had no idea about the IRMAA costs associated with Medicare. That little mistake cost my client an extra $8,000 in Medicare costs for he and his wife, of which he was unaware. After this disaster, I started to educate myself about all-things-taxes and Medicare so that I would never make a mistake like that again. A major part of an effective retirement plan involves what you just learned.

Managing your money is one part of retirement planning. Think of it as the gas that fuels your car. Managing your taxes, income, goals, expectations, and emotions are the most important parts of retirement planning; this is like the engine in your car. I'm a pro at filling up my car, most people can do that. And I can tell you where the engine is, but that's about it. Thousands of financial advisors out there want to manage your money (the easy part), but great advisors will consider all aspects of your financial lives. Those are the ones you should find to work with.

This last part is filled with some of the very important aspects of your retirement plan. If you currently have a plan in place and you have not addressed all these concepts, you don't have a complete financial plan. You have an investment strategy.

From all this information in this book you now have the tools to create your own "RedZone Retirement Plan." What you do from here is up to you.

CHAPTER 14

PICKING YOUR TEAM

> "Look, I don't really know where we should take this bus. But I know this much: If we get the right people on the bus, the right people in the right seats, and the wrong people off the bus, then we'll figure out how to take it someplace great."
>
> ~ JAMES C. COLLINS, AMERICAN RESEARCHER, AUTHOR, AND SPEAKER

Now that you have your "Retirement RedZone Plan" you need to decide on how you will execute. Are you going to do it yourself? If so, use some of the online tools that I mentioned in the book to drill down the exact details of your plan. If you do this yourself, I encourage you at a minimum to have a consultation with a CFP about your plan to make sure you are on the right track. This second opinion will also be useful to point out any holes in your plan.

If you want to use a team, who do you use? How do you decide who to use, and why?

I'm a big proponent of the team approach to retirement planning, because you are certain to have some unknowns pop up in your retirement. You will have a need to call an audible or two during your time in the RedZone. Having a team to fall back on when something doesn't go your way gives you a great amount of peace. In our office, we like to think of ourselves as your Chief Financial Officer (CFO), with you being the Chief Executive Officer (CEO). CEOs have a need to delegate some of the tasks that they are not good at or that they don't have time for. That is exactly where we come in. We coordinate all areas of your financial life to make sure that we are firing on all cylinders. Think of us as your financial quarterbacks, we are calling plays and audibles to get the WIN for you in your retirement.

The principles for success are the same for investing as for any other business. You are the CEO, you can think of us as your CFO.

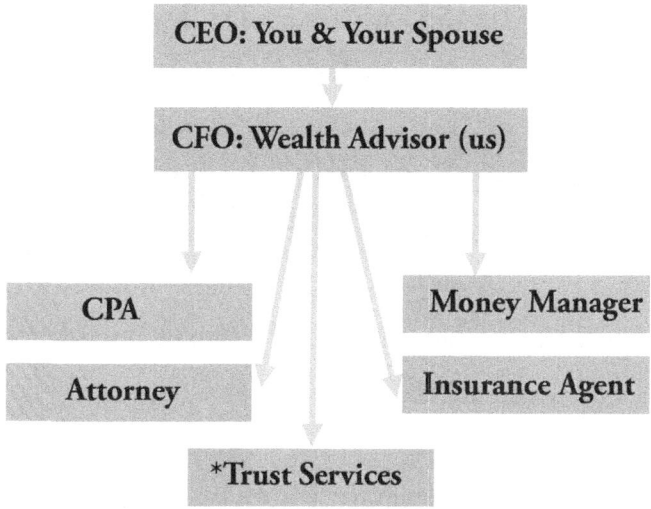

*Securities offered through Mutual of Omaha Investor Services, Inc. a Registered Broker/Dealer, Member FINRA/SIPC. Advisory services offered through Mutual of Omaha Investor Services, Inc. a SEC Registered Investment Advisory Firm. Please refer to Mutual of Omaha Investor Services, Inc. Form ADV Part 2 brochures for a more detailed explanation of the financial planning and advisory services offered. These brochures disclose information about the qualifications and business practices of the firm as well as the services provided, disciplinary actions, outside business activities, and potential conflicts of interest. Mutual of Omaha Investor Services, Inc. and its representatives do not provide tax or legal advice. Consult the appropriate professional regarding your particular situation. *Trust services offered through an associated third party provider.

Here is a great example of a situation where you will need to call an audible.

Almost half of people who retire do so earlier than they expected because of health issues of their own, health issues of a spouse, or because of job loss.[14]

That could throw a huge wrench in your retirement plan, and you will need to make some adjustments to account for that. Having a CFP that you are working with can quickly make some adjustments to counteract this unknown. If you are doing this on your own, and you are forced into an early retirement, I would assume a large amount of stress will start to set in fast. Having a trusted partner that you can rely on will take a huge amount of stress of your back.

I find that many clients gain confidence and peace of mind when they work with a financial advisor on their retirement plan. In fact, baby boomers who work with a financial advisor are twice as likely to feel confident about their retirement savings, this is compared to baby boomers who don't work with an advisor. The two biggest concerns that advisors addressed for these clients were: the fear of running out of money and protecting principal. I think we have talked about those enough in this book to make you aware that these are two major things that we focus on in the "RedZone Retirement Plan."

Personal finance is WAY more *personal* than it is **finance**. Everyone's situation is unique, and retirement planning is not one size fits all. Often, I find myself feeling like a counselor during our client meetings. We spend way more time on the emotional side of retirement than we do with the numbers. The numbers are what they are, but your emotional self is what I find needs the most care during this RedZone period.

Sure, sequence of returns matter, and withdrawal rates matter, but your emotions matter as well.

A good financial planner should help you with tax issues, investment options, emotional decisions, Medicare coverages, and your overall plan. I highly suggest you research your advisor before you hire them and interview a few different advisors to see who you best gel with. Most of us don't marry the first person that we date. Date a few advisors/firms to see who you fit the best with; don't be afraid to test the waters. Some questions for you to ask your advisor can be found in the Deliverables section at the back of my books.

When we are interviewing clients to work with, we love clients that have these following characteristics:

- Wanting and needing help and willing to delegate the work to us.
- Willing to take advice from us.
- Have similar values as our firm. (Listed in the Deliverables)
- Basic understanding of the strategy and process that we have in place.
- Have realistic goals and expectations for their investments and lifestyle.
- We enjoy working together, and it is beneficial for all parties.

Some people in the financial services industry that say they are "Financial Advisors" are just salespeople selling a product. I would prefer that you find an advisor who is a CFP, so visit *www.letsmakeaplan.org*. You will find a ton of advisors who are not CFPs who are great at what they do and put your interest first. The CFP marks simply show that the advisor is well versed in all things personal finance and holds themselves to a higher standard. You should also check your advisor out on *www.Brokercheck.finra.org* this will show any past legal action against them.

The U.S. has around 92,000 CFPs in 2020. By contrast, there are more than 1,100,000 stockbrokers, insurance agents, and financial advisors. Making sure one of the non-CFPs is a good one can be a complicated task. If in your initial interview with the advisor all they want to talk about is your money and investments, there is a pretty good chance they may be out to just make a sale. On the other hand, if they take time to get to know you and what your goals are, they may have your best interest in mind.

This book did give you some general rules of thumb and some guidelines for you to consider when setting up your retirement distribution plan. I do want to stress to you that these are **general** statements, and everyone's situation is completely different. Your retirement has many variables that go into it, developing a one size fits all plan is near impossible.

Saying that there is one financial plan that is best for everyone is like taking the standard American diet, which hovers around 2100-2500 daily calories depending on a few factors, and applying that to everyone without regard for their lifestyle, health, activity level, etc.

I had a knee injury early in 2022, and I didn't want to gain a bunch of weight, so I started to track my calories. I remember the first day I hit 4,000 calories when I entered everything at the end of the day. I was a little shocked and concerned with my caloric intake after looking at "the standard," but after a month I averaged 3,800 calories a day and didn't gain any weight. My caloric intake is quite a bit more than the "standard" diet. The food you eat and your activity level are a few of the variables in determining how many calories you should eat for your goals. I would say your retirement plan has at least 10 times more variables than your diet does. So, make sure you get a plan that is tailored to fit your personal needs.

If you don't get expert advice and get a proper plan in place you could underestimate your retirement income needs, which could have drastic life altering consequences. I would highly encourage you to, at a minimum, get a second opinion from a professional if you are doing this yourself. Guidelines are great, but everyone's plan will be different.

You have the tools now to create your own "RedZone Retirement Plan." What you do and where you go from here is up to you. Best of luck to you in your retirement planning. Listed in the Deliverables are some key take aways that I wanted to illustrate to you.

If you need help or a consultation, our office is here to assist you in any way we can. We can be reached at 402-379-6745, *www.adamolson.biz*, or *adam.olson@mutualofomaha.com*. We work with clients in our physical offices and virtually around the country.

Disclosures:

> *A note about the strategies discussed in this book. The author does not guarantee the accuracy or completeness of the information presented herein. Information is subject to change without notice. The information presented is generic in nature not intended as an offer or solicitation with respect to the purchase or sale of any security or insurance product. The strategies or opinions presented are*

not meant as individual investment advice and may not be suitable for everyone.

You should carefully consider all your available options prior to making any financial decisions. Be sure to understand the benefits and limitations of your available options and consider factors such as differences in fees and expenses, available investment options, loan provisions, distribution options, tax treatment, and other concerns specific to your individual circumstances. Consult with a professional tax and/or legal advisor before taking any action that may have tax or legal consequences.

Mutual of Omaha Investor Services, Inc. does not provide tax or legal advice. Please consult with the appropriate professional regarding your personal situation prior to making any financial decisions.

Securities and advisory services offered through Mutual of Omaha Investor Services, Inc Member FINRA/SIPC Adam Olson, Representative

Deliverables:
Questions to ask a Financial Advisor:

These are some questions you should be asking when you interview a financial advisor that you potentially want to work with.

1. What do you love about your job?

- Find out what there "why" is. Why do they do what they do? What drives them?

2. Are you a fiduciary?

- This is a simple yes or no answer. An Advisor that is a fiduciary is legally obligated to put your interest above their own. So, a Yes answer to this is good. If no, then you need to dig into why they are not? What standard or code do they abide by?

3. How do you get paid, and what are my "all in" costs?

- Make sure to ask "all in" total costs. The Financial Advisor's fees are only part of the cost you will incur to work with them. You may also have platform fees and mutual fund fees.

4. How are you qualified to serve me, and what credentials do you hold?

- How long have they been in the business? Are they continually educating themselves and keep up with trends?

5. What is your investment philosophy?
- See if they can even answer this one. Do they believe in stock picking or a passively managed fund?

6. What services do you provide?
- Does the Advisor also sell insurance and do tax prep work?
  If so, how do they get paid, and what does that cost?

7. How do you measure and evaluate the success of our relationship?
- What benchmarks or goals do they have to determine if your relationship is successful?

8. How often do we meet, and what are my responsibilities?
- Look for a structured plan of meetings and follow ups. Make sure you know what you are required to do in the relationship.

9. Have you been subject to disciplinary or legal actions?

- Has the advisor ever been sued by a client? I would also make sure they are licensed and appointed with the proper agencies. Go to brokercheck.finra.org to find out for sure.

10. What's your succession plan if something were to happen to you?

- What happens to your account if the advisor dies or gets out of the business?

Effect of Inflation

Over the last 54 years, the average annual inflation rate in the U.S. has been 3.76%.[1]

Item Description	Value
Annual inflation rate	3.00%
Number of years from now	30
Current item cost	$100
Future item cost	**$243**

Example

Assuming an average annual inflation rate of 3.00%, an item which costs $100 today will cost $243 in 30 year(s).

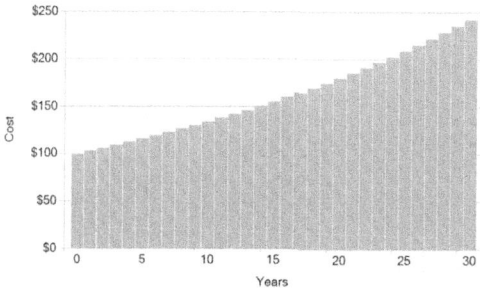

[1] Source: U.S. Bureau of Labor Statistics, Consumer Price Index for Urban Wage Earners and Clerical Workers (CPI-W); U.S. City Average. 1967-2021.

A349X

Asset Allocation Questionnaire

Instructions: Answer the following questions. Then add your scores for each question and match your total score with the corresponding portfolio type shown at the end of the questionnaire. Please consult with your investment representative to make sure the results are consistent with your needs and investment personality, and for help in selecting specific investment choices that are suitable for you.

Time Horizon

Q1. In how many years do you expect to begin making withdrawals from your investment account?
- ☐ Immediately (1 point)
- ☐ Within the next 3 years (3 points)
- ☐ 3 to 6 years (6 points)
- ☐ 6 to 10 years (9 points)
- ☐ 10 to 15 years (12 points)
- ☐ More than 15 years (15 points)

Q2. How long do you expect withdrawals from your investment account to continue?
- ☐ I expect to take a lump sum (1 point)
- ☐ Under 3 years (3 points)
- ☐ 3 to 6 years (6 points)
- ☐ 6 to 10 years (9 points)
- ☐ 10 to 15 years (12 points)
- ☐ More than 15 years (15 points)

Risk Tolerance

Q3. Which statement best describes your investment objective for your investment account?
- ☐ I am looking for stability of my account balance and want to avoid any losses. (1 point)
- ☐ I am looking for stability of my account, but I can accept a low to moderate amount of fluctuation in my account if I can have more growth potential. (3 points)
- ☐ I am focused on growth. I am not concerned about moderate fluctuations each year. (6 points)
- ☐ I am focused on account growth, and I am willing to accept a higher level of risk for higher returns. (9 points)
- ☐ I am seeking the most growth possible, and I am not concerned about fluctuations in the value of my account. (12 points)
- ☐ I am not sure what my investment objective should be. (3 points)

Q4. Which statement best describes your approach as an investor?
- ☐ I am very cautious about taking risks, and I want to avoid losses in my account. (1 point)
- ☐ I am somewhat cautious about taking risks, and I can handle relatively small losses in my account occasionally. (3 points)
- ☐ I am mixed between taking risks that are generally associated with greater account growth potential and the desire to minimize short-term losses in my account. (6 points)
- ☐ I am open to taking some risks for growth potential. I am less concerned about short-term (less than one year) losses or gains; I am looking more for long-term growth in my investments. (9 points)
- ☐ I am a risk taker, and want to maximize the growth of my account over the next decade or longer, and am not concerned about short-term losses. (12 points)
- ☐ I am not sure what type of investor I am. (3 points)

Q5. Generally, I'm very impatient during unfavorable market conditions, and will usually change my mind often.
- ☐ I strongly agree (1 point)
- ☐ I agree (3 points)
- ☐ I somewhat agree (5 points)
- ☐ I disagree (7 points)
- ☐ I strongly disagree (11 points)
- ☐ I'm not sure (3 points)

Q6. Consider the following ranges of possible returns over a one-year period. Which set of possibilities are you most comfortable with as it relates to your investment account?
☐ A (1 point)   ☐ B (2 points)   ☐ C (3 points)   ☐ D (4 points)   ☐ E (5 points)

	Low	Average	High
A.	-2.0%	6.4%	17.3%
B.	-5.6%	7.8%	22.3%
C.	-10.2%	9.2%	30.8%
D.	-16.4%	10.2%	38.9%
E.	-22.5%	11.1%	46.9%

The ranges in the table are based on historical returns of different allocations of stocks and bonds, as represented by appropriate indices, over the last 76 years. The table reflects the range of returns an investor could have experienced 95 percent of the time in any one-year. These ranges are intended for the purpose of assessing risk tolerance and determining investment suitability. They do not represent the actual historical returns of any particular investment fund or vehicle, nor are they a prediction or guarantee of future investment performance.

MC33029

Q7. The chart below shows possible growth of $40,000 over a five-year period for a series of different investment strategies. Which of the five scenarios are you most comfortable with as an investor?
☐ A (1 point) ☐ B (2 points) ☐ C (3 points) ☐ D (4 points) ☐ E (5 points)

A. $44,476   AVERAGE $54,624 $73,301
B. $41,376   AVERAGE $58,123 $80,084
C. $38,024   AVERAGE $61,998 $88,148
D. $32,937   AVERAGE $65,126 $98,855
E. $27,514   AVERAGE $67,646 $112,629

The ranges in the table are based on historical returns of different allocations of stocks and bonds, as represented by appropriate indices, over the last 76 years. The dollar amounts illustrate what could happen 95 percent of the time after five years if an investor had an initial investment of $40,000. These ranges are intended for the purpose of assessing risk tolerance and determining investment suitability. They do not represent the actual historical returns of any particular investment fund or vehicle, nor are they a prediction or guarantee of future investment performance.

Q8. What would you do if you heard on the news or read in the newspaper that the U.S. stock market suddenly dropped by 20%?

☐ I would change my strategy to something with less volatility. This kind of market volatility makes me very nervous – I don't want to be exposed to this type of risk again. (1 point)

☐ I would move most of my account into something a bit less risky. This kind of market volatility makes me nervous, but I would consider getting back into stock funds when it has quieted down. (4 points)

☐ I would probably move half of my stock portfolio balance into something with less market volatility, such as cash or bonds. This kind of market volatility makes me a little nervous, so I would rather reduce some of my stock exposure until the market has quieted down. (7 points)

☐ I would stick with my investments, but I would probably worry about meeting my investment goals and watch my account balance very closely. (10 points)

☐ I would stick with my investment selections and would not make any changes. I have enough time and patience to ride it out. (13 points)

☐ I don't know what I would do. (4 points)

Scoring and Corresponding Model Portfolio

Q1) _____   Q5) _____
Q2) _____   Q6) _____
Q3) _____   Q7) _____
Q4) _____   Q8) _____

            Total Points _____

Scores Between:
  8 and 18 >   **Conservative**
  19 and 38 > **Moderately Conservative**
  39 and 58 > **Moderate**
  59 and 78 > **Moderately Aggressive**
  79 and 88 > **Aggressive**

Investor Name: _____   Representative Name: _____

Signature: _____   Signature: _____

Date: _____

PICKING YOUR TEAM

Do You Desire "Retirement Peace of Mind?"

In December 2012, a landmark study was launched to determine a national retirement peace of mind.[1] It included more than 6,000 respondents age 45 and older. It found that average Americans have a lot of challenges and a lot of expectations for their retirement years.

Retirement Expectations

Traditionally, many Americans have viewed retirement as a time of leisure. Today, more and more of us expect to work during our retirement years. Seven out of ten of those surveyed in the study said that their ideal plan for balancing work and leisure in retirement would be to include some work.

The reasons are not purely economic. Many Americans see retirement as a time for renewal and accomplishment. When asked if they would seek the same kind of work in retirement or pursue a different career, half of those surveyed said they would seek a different line of work.

A desire for more money and economic security was the most important reason for working in retirement according to a majority of the survey participants, but 48 percent said a desire for stimulation and satisfaction was their top reason for continuing to work during retirement.

When asked about their most important financial goal, 88 percent said they would like to save enough money to have financial peace of mind, versus 12% who said they would like to accumulate as much wealth as possible.

Retirement Challenges

The study also sought information on the greatest concerns facing those nearing retirement. Not surprisingly, in today's complex economic and social climate, they found many complications that could make the task of retirement planning even more challenging.

- **Health problems**: Americans are expected to live longer than ever before. When asked what concerned them about living a long life, 72% of those surveyed said they feared serious health problems, making it the top retirement worry. This compares with 47% who said they worried they would run out of the money they need to live a comfortable retirement.

There is good reason for concern. The study found that the top reason for early retirement given by those already retired was due to personal health problems. Fully 57% of study participants who had already retired reported they retired earlier than they had planned.

- **Caring for family members**: More and more Americans today are left caring for others in their families: adult children, grandchildren, parents or in-laws, siblings. These Americans are often referred to as the "Sandwich Generation", finding their own needs for saving and retirement security squeezed by the needs of others they love.

Among study participants aged 45 or older with children, over half said they expected to have to continue to provide support to adult children. More than a third expected to have to support grandchildren. Fewer said they expected to have to support parents (16%) or their siblings (10%).

The types of support they expected to provide included financial support (cash or loans), housing (sharing a home or helping pay for housing), education and healthcare. The study also found a relationship between income and expectations for providing support: participants with higher incomes were two times more likely to say they expected to provide support to their adult children, grandchildren and parents than those with lower incomes.

Do You Have "Retirement Peace of Mind?"

The study tried to determine how close participants were to achieving retirement peace of mind by asking them to respond to these survey questions:

Question
• I feel content and comfortable about how I will spend my retirement years.
• I have many worries about what might happen during my retirement.
• Thinking about my retirement gives me feelings of security and stability.
• I feel anxious and uneasy about how I will support myself and my family during retirement.
• I feel well prepared for whatever may happen during my retirement.

Do You Desire "Retirement Peace of Mind?"

The study found that participants had an average score of 5.3, based on a scale of 1 to 10, or slightly above average. Scores varied, though, by gender, the amount of savings, and if the participant worked with a financial professional.

- Men were more likely than women to have retirement peace of mind. The average score for male participants was 5.6 while female participants averaged 5.0.

- Participants with $500,000 or more in investable savings averaged a score of 7.5 while those with under $250,000 in investable savings averaged 4.8.

- Participants who worked with a financial professional at the time of the study had an average score of 6.3, while those who did not work with a financial professional had a score of 4.7.

How Can You Improve Your Retirement Peace of Mind?

The results of the national study suggest several steps you can take today to improve your peace of mind during retirement:

- What is your most important financial goal? Are you like the 88 percent who said they would like to save enough money to have financial peace of mind? Or, are you more like the 12% who said they would like to accumulate as much wealth as possible? The answer may help determine your retirement savings and investment strategy.

- Do you intend to work during retirement? Will you stay in the same line of work, or start a new career… maybe even a business of your own? If you do intend to work, it could affect the Social Security benefits for which you qualify. You will want to research the impact carefully.

- What will you do for personal satisfaction? While a desire for more income and security was the top reason for working in retirement, almost half of the study participants said they intended to do so for personal stimulation and satisfaction. What will you do for stimulation and satisfaction? Do you wish to travel? Start a new career? Volunteer in your community? Whatever your choices, look carefully to see how they may affect your retirement savings goals. Do you need to save money to start a business? To complete a college education? To travel?

- **Are you prepared for any personal healthcare issues that could arise?** Problems with personal health lead more people to retire earlier than planned more than any other cause. Do you understand your medical care and long-term care options? Does your employer offer extended healthcare benefits to retirees or will you be required to provide your own? Is disability insurance appropriate for your situation?

- **Do you have any other family obligations to consider?** More and more retirees today find they must continue to provide financial support for their adult children, grandchildren, parents or siblings. Are you supporting family members today? Do you intend to support family members during retirement? How is supporting family today affecting your ability to save for retirement? Are there other strategies you should consider? Is life insurance something you should consider to help care for survivors or heirs?

- **Would you benefit from professional financial advice?** Participants in the nation-wide study reported overall higher levels of retirement peace of mind when they worked with a financial professional. Would discussing your retirement goals and challenges with a professional help you?

Whatever your expectations for retirement, like all important things in life, it pays to have a plan to achieve them and to regularly measure your progress towards your goals.

Secure Act 2.0 changes

The Secure Act 2.0 was signed into law late December 2022. This law made some major changes to RMD's, increasing contribution limits in retirement accounts, and other changes to help people save for retirement.

Quick Highlights:

- The age to start taking RMDs increases to 73 in 2023 and to 75 in 2033.

- Catch-up contributions will increase in 2025 for 401(k), 403(b), governmental plans, and IRAs.

- New provisions for rolling a 529 Plan to a Roth IRA.

- Updates to Qualified Charitable Distributions, QDC's.

- Addition of Roth Contributions in SIMPLE IRA's.

The changes are far more expansive then this short list, and not feasible to be covered in detail. For specifics on the Secure Act 2.0 please visit IRS.GOV or speak with your CPA.

APPENDIX

1. Team Tony. (n.d.) *Discover the 6 human needs.* Retrieved from *https://www.tonyrobbins.com/mind-meaning/do-you-need-to-feel-significant/*

2. Jason, J. (14, November 2021). *Still working after age 65 and thinking of moving?* Retrieved from *https://www.forbes.com/sites/juliejason/2021/11/14/still-working-after-age-65-and--thinking-of-moving/?sh=16a90df45402*

3. Purcell, P. (December 2015). *Income taxes on social security benefits.* Retrieved from *https://www.ssa.gov/policy/docs/issuepapers/ip2015-02.html*

4. Longtermcare.gov. (18, February 2020). *How much care will you need?* Retrieved from *https://acl.gov/ltc/basic-needs/how-much-care-will-you-need*

5. Genworth.com. (n.d.). *Cost of care survey.* Retrieved from *https://www.genworth.com/aging-and-you/finances/cost-of-care.html*

6. IRS.gov. (n.d.). *Are my social security or railroad retirement tier 1 benefits taxable?* Retrieved from *https://www.irs.gov/help/ita/are-my-social-security-or-railroad-retirement-tier-i-benefits-taxable*

7. SSA.gov. (n.d.). *Income taxes and your social security benefits.* Retrieved from *https://www.ssa.gov/benefits/retirement/planner/taxes.html*

8. SSA.gov. (n.d.). *Receiving benefits while working.* Retrieved from *https://www.ssa.gov/benefits/retirement/planner/whileworking.html*

9. CMS.gov. (27, September 2022). *2023 medicare parts a & b premiums and deductibles…* Retrieved from *https://www.cms.gov/newsroom/fact-sheets/2023-medicare-parts-b-premiums-and-deductibles-2023-medicare-part-d-income-related-monthly*

10. Medicare.gov. (n.d.). *Monthly premiums for drug plans.* Retrieved from *https://www.medicare.gov/drug-coverage-part-d/costs-for-medicare-drug-coverage/monthly-premium-for-drug-plans*

11. IRS.gov. (n.d.). *Questions and answers on the net investment income tax.* Retrieved from *https://www.irs.gov/newsroom/questions-and-answers-on-the-net-investment-income-tax*

12. Mengle, R. (3, November 2022). *What are the capital tax gains rates for 2022 vs. 2023?* Retrieved from *https://www.kiplinger.com/taxes/capital-gains-tax/602224/capital-gains-tax-rates*

13. Smartasset.com. (n.d.). *What are the best states to retire for taxes?* Retrieved from *https://smartasset.com/retirement/retirement-taxes*

14. Murillo, A. (4, May 2021). *You'll probably have to retire earlier than planned…* Retrieved from *https://money.com/early-retirement-how-to-save/*

THE REASON I DO WHAT I DO

Made in the USA
Monee, IL
15 May 2023